ECONOMICS

ECONOMICS

•

Partha Dasgupta

A BRIEF INSIGHT

STERLING

New York / London
www.sterlingpublishing.com

STERLING and the distinctive Sterling logo are registered trademarks of
Sterling Publishing Co., Inc.

Library of Congress Cataloging-in-Publication Data

Dasgupta, Partha.
  Economics : a very short introduction / Partha Dasgupta.
    p. cm. -- (A brief insight)
  Originally published: Oxford ; New York : Oxford University Press, 2007.
  Includes bibliographical references and index.
  ISBN 978-1-4027-6894-1
  1. Economics. I. Title.
  HB171.D26 2010
  330--dc22
                                2009037985

10 9 8 7 6 5 4 3 2 1

Published by Sterling Publishing Co., Inc.
387 Park Avenue South, New York, NY 10016

Published by arrangement with Oxford University Press, Inc.

© 2007 by Partha Dasgupta
Illustrated edition published in 2010 by Sterling Publishing Co., Inc.
Additional text © 2010 Sterling Publishing Co., Inc.

Distributed in Canada by Sterling Publishing
c/o Canadian Manda Group, 165 Dufferin Street
Toronto, Ontario, Canada M6K 3H6

Book design: The DesignWorks Group

Please see picture credits on page 212 for image copyright information.

Sterling ISBN 978-1-4027-6894-1

For information about custom editions, special sales, premium and
corporate purchases, please contact Sterling Special Sales
Department at 800-805-5489 or specialsales@sterlingpublishing.com.

Frontispiece: Shoppers browse for Chinese New Year gifts at a bazaar in Qingdao, a city in China's
Shandong province.

CONTENTS

•

Preface VII

Prologue I

ONE   Macroeconomic History 17

TWO   Trust 39

THREE Communities 81

FOUR Markets 91

FIVE Science and Technology as Institutions........................... 113

SIX Households and Firms 125

SEVEN Sustainable Economic Development 147

EIGHT Social Well-being and Democratic Government............... 175

Epilogue 201

Further Reading 204

Index 206

Picture Credits 212

PREFACE

·

WRITING AN INTRODUCTION TO economics is both easy and hard. It's easy because in one way or another we are all economists. No one, for example, has to explain to us what prices are—we face them every day. Experts may have to explain why banks offer interest on saving deposits or why risk aversion is a tricky concept or why the way we measure wealth misses much of the point of measuring it, but none of these is an alien idea. As economics matters to us, we also have views on what should be done to put things right when we feel they are wrong. And we hold our views strongly because our ethics drive our politics and our politics inform our economics. When thinking economics we don't entertain doubts. So, the very reasons we want to study economics act as stumbling blocks even as we try to uncover the pathways by which the economic world gets shaped. But as economics is in large measure *about* those pathways—it's as evidence-based a social science as is possible—it shouldn't be surprising that most often disagreements people have over economic issues are, ultimately, about their reading of "facts," not about the "values" they hold. Which is why writing an introduction to economics is hard.

When I first drew up plans to write this book, I had it in mind to offer readers an overview of economics as it appears in leading economics journals and textbooks. But even though the analytical and empirical core of economics has grown from strength to strength over the decades, I haven't been at ease with the selection of topics that textbooks offer for discussion (rural life in poor regions—that is, the economic life of some 2.5 billion people—doesn't get mentioned at all), nor with the subjects that are emphasized in leading economics journals (Nature rarely appears there as an active player). It also came home to me that Oxford University Press had asked me to write *a very short* introduction to economics and there are economics textbooks that are over 1,000 pages long! So it struck me that I should abandon my original plan and offer an account of the *reasoning* we economists apply in order to understand the social world around us and then deploy that reasoning to some of the most urgent problems Humanity faces today. It's only recently that I realized that I would be able to do that only if I shaped the discourse round the lives of my two literary grandchildren—Becky and Desta. Becky's and Desta's lives are as different as they can be, but as they are both *my* grandchildren, I believe I understand them. More importantly, economics has helped me to understand them.

The ideas developed here were framed and explored in my book, *An Inquiry into Well-Being and Destitution* (Oxford: Clarendon Press, 1993). While writing that book I realized that economics had increasingly driven my ethics and that my ethics in turn had informed my politics. As that is an unusual causal chain, the earlier book was more technical and a lot "heavier." Theoretical and empirical advances since it was published have led me to hold the viewpoint I advanced there even more strongly now. I understand things much better than I did then—including *why* I don't understand many things. The present work is a natural extension of my earlier book.

While preparing this monograph I have benefited greatly from correspondence and discussions with Kenneth Arrow, Gretchen Daily, Carol Dasgupta, Paul Ehrlich, Petra Geraats, Lawrence Goulder, Timothy Gowers, Rashid Hassan, Sriya Iyer, Pramila Krishnan, Simon Levin, Karl-Göran Mäler, Eric Maskin, Pranab Mukhopadhay, Kevin Mumford, Richard Nolan, Sheilagh Ogilvie, Kirsten Oleson, Alaknanda Patel, Subhrendu Pattanaik, William Peterson, Hamid Sabourian, Dan Schrag, Priya Shyamsundar, Jeff Vincent, Martin Weale, and Gavin Wright. The present version reflects the impact of the comments I received on an earlier draft from Kenneth Arrow, Carol Dasgupta, Geoffrey Harcourt, Mike Shaw, Robert Solow, and Sylvana Tomaselli. Sue Pilkington has helped me in innumerable ways to prepare the book for publication. I am grateful to them all.

St. John's College
Cambridge
August 2006

PROLOGUE

•

Becky's World

BECKY, WHO IS TEN YEARS OLD, lives with her parents and an older brother Sam in a suburban town in America's Midwest. Becky's father works in a firm specializing in property law. Depending on the firm's profits, his annual income varies somewhat, but is rarely below US $145,000. Becky's parents met at college. For a few years her mother worked in publishing, but when Sam was born she decided to concentrate on raising a family. Now that both Becky and Sam attend school, she does voluntary work in local education. The family lives in a two-story house. It has four bedrooms, two bathrooms upstairs and a toilet downstairs, a large drawing-cum-dining room, a modern kitchen, and a family

There are striking contrasts in poverty and wealth across the globe. While Desta's Ethiopian family lives in a grass-thatched mud hut, Becky's American family occupies a spacious home composed of industrially processed materials: vinyl siding, asphalt shingles, fiberglass insulation, and poured concrete.

room in the basement. There is a plot of land at the rear—the backyard—which the family uses for leisure activities.

Although their property is partially mortgaged, Becky's parents own stocks and bonds and have a saving account in the local branch of a national bank. Becky's father and his firm jointly contribute to his retirement pension. He also makes monthly payments into a scheme with the bank that will cover college education for Becky and Sam. The family's assets and their lives are insured. Becky's parents often remark that, because federal

Ten-year-old Becky rides her bike to school.

taxes are high, they have to be careful with money; and they are. Nevertheless, they own two cars; the children attend camp each summer; and the family takes a vacation together once camp is over. Becky's parents also remark that her generation will be much more prosperous than theirs. Becky wants to save the environment and insists on biking to school. Her ambition is to become a doctor.

Desta's World

Desta, who is about ten years old, lives with her parents and five siblings in a village in subtropical, southwest Ethiopia. The family lives in a two-room, grass-roofed mud hut. Desta's father grows maize and *teff* (a staple cereal unique to Ethiopia) on half a hectare of land that the government has awarded him. Desta's older brother helps him to farm the land and care for the household's livestock, which consist of a cow, a goat, and a few chickens. The small quantity of *teff* produced is sold so as to raise cash income, but the maize is in large measure consumed by the household as a staple. Desta's mother works a small plot next to their cottage, growing cabbage, onions, and *enset* (a year-round root crop that also serves as a staple). In order to supplement their household income, she brews a local drink made from maize. As she is also responsible for cooking, cleaning, and minding the infants, her work day usually lasts fourteen hours. Despite the long hours, it wouldn't be possible for her to complete the tasks on her own. (As the ingredients are all raw, cooking alone takes five hours or more.) So Desta and her older sister help their mother with household chores and mind their younger siblings. Although a younger brother attends the local school, neither Desta nor her older sister has ever been enrolled there. Her parents can neither read nor write, but they are numerate.

Desta's home has no electricity or running water. Around where they live, sources of water, land for grazing cattle, and the woodlands are communal property. They are shared by people in Desta's village; but the villagers don't allow outsiders to make use of them. Each day Desta's mother and the girls fetch water, collect fuel wood, and pick berries and herbs from the local commons. Desta's mother frequently complains that the time and effort needed to collect their daily needs has increased over the years.

There is no financial institution nearby to offer either credit or insurance. As funerals are expensive occasions, Desta's father long ago joined a community insurance scheme (*iddir*) to which he contributes monthly. When Desta's father purchased the cow they now own, he used the entire cash he had accumulated and stored at home, but had to supplement that with funds borrowed from kinfolk, with a promise to

Ten-year-old Desta does not attend school, but spends her day carrying out household chores alongside her mother and older sister. Here, in Debre Markos, Ethiopia, two sisters gather cattle dung to be used for fuel.

repay the debt when he had the ability to do so. In turn, when they are in need, his kinfolk come to him for a loan, which he supplies if he is able to. Desta's father says that such patterns of reciprocity he and those close to him practice are part of their culture. He says also that his sons are his main assets, as they are the ones who will look after him and Desta's mother in their old age.

Economic statisticians estimate that, adjusting for differences in the cost of living between Ethiopia and the United States (US), Desta's family income is about $5,500 per year, of which $1,100 are attributable to the products they draw from the local commons. However, as rainfall varies from year to year, Desta's family income fluctuates widely. In bad years, the grain they store at home gets depleted well before the next harvest. Food is then so scarce that they all grow weaker, the younger children especially so. It is only after harvest that they regain their weight and strength. Periodic hunger and illnesses have meant that Desta and her siblings are somewhat stunted. Over the years Desta's parents have lost two children in their infancy, stricken by malaria in one case and diarrhea in the other. There have also been several miscarriages.

Desta knows that she will be married (in all likelihood to a farmer, like her father) five years from now and will then live on her husband's land in a neighboring village. She expects her life to be similar to that of her mother.

The Economist's Agenda

That the lives people are able to construct differ enormously across the globe is a commonplace. In our age of travel, it is even a common sight. That Becky and Desta face widely different futures is also something we have come to expect, perhaps also to accept. Nevertheless, it may not be out of turn to imagine that the girls are intrinsically very similar. They both enjoy playing, eating, and gossiping; they are close to their families; they turn to their mothers when in distress; they like pretty things to wear; and they both have the capacity to be disappointed, get annoyed, and be happy.

Their parents are also alike. They are knowledgeable about the ways of their worlds. They also care about their families, finding ingenious ways to meet the recurring problem of producing income and allocating resources among family members—over time and allowing for unexpected contingencies. So, a promising route for exploring the underlying causes behind their vastly different conditions of life would be to begin by observing that the opportunities and obstacles the families face are very different, that in some sense Desta's family are far more restricted in what they are able to be and do than Becky's.

Economics in great measure tries to uncover the processes that influence how people's lives come to be what they are. The discipline also tries to identify ways to influence those very processes so as to improve the prospects of those who are hugely constrained in what they can be and do. The former activity involves finding explanations, while the latter tries to identify policy prescriptions. Economists also make forecasts of what the conditions of economic life are going to be; but if the predictions are to be taken seriously, they have to be built on an understanding of the processes that shape people's lives; which is why the attempt to explain takes precedence over forecasting.

The context in which explanations are sought or in which prescriptions are made could be a household, a village, a district, a country, or even the whole world—the extent to which people or places are aggregated merely reflects the details with which we choose to study the social world. Imagine that we wish to understand the basis on which food is shared among household members in a community. Household income would no doubt be expected to play a role; but we would need to look inside households if we are to discover whether food is allocated on the basis of age, gender, and status. If we find that it is, we should ask why they play a role and what policy prescriptions, if any, commend themselves. In contrast, suppose we want to know whether the world as a whole is wealthier today than it was fifty years ago. As the question is about global averages, we would be justified in ironing out differences within and among households.

Averaging is required over time as well. The purpose of the study and the cost of collecting information influence the choice of the unit of time over which the averaging is done. The population census in India, for example, is conducted every ten years. More frequent censuses would be more costly and wouldn't yield extra information of any great importance. In contrast, if we are to study changes in the volume of home sales across seasons, even annual statistics would miss the point of the inquiry. Monthly statistics on home sales are a favorite compromise between detail and the cost of obtaining detail.

Modern economics, by which I mean the style of economics taught and practiced in today's leading universities, likes to start the inquiries from the ground up: from individuals, through the household,

A US census taker interviews a farmer on a horse-drawn farm machine in 1940. Information garnered from periodic censuses is crucial to the economist's work.

village, district, state, country, to the whole world. In various degrees, the millions of individual decisions shape the eventualities people face; as both theory, common sense, and evidence tell us that there are enormous numbers of consequences of what we all do. Some of those consequences have been intended, but many are unintended. There is, however, a feedback, in that those consequences in turn go to shape what people subsequently can do and choose to do. When Becky's family drive their cars or use electricity, or when Desta's family create compost or burn wood for cooking, they add to global carbon emissions. Their contributions are no doubt negligible, but the millions of such tiny contributions sum to a sizeable amount, having consequences that people everywhere are likely to experience in different ways. It can be that the feedbacks are positive, so that the whole contribution is greater than the sum of the parts. Strikingly, unintended consequences can include emergent features, such as market prices, at which the demand for goods more or less equals their supply.

Earlier, I gave a description of Becky's and Desta's lives. *Understanding* their lives involves a lot more; it requires analysis, which usually calls for further description. To conduct an analysis, we need first of all to identify the material prospects the girls' households face—now and in the future, under uncertain contingencies. Second, we need to uncover the character of their choices and the pathways by which the choices made by millions of households like Becky's and Desta's go to produce the prospects they all face. Third, we need to uncover the pathways by which the families came to inherit their current circumstances.

These amount to a tall, even forbidding, order. Moreover, there is a thought that can haunt us: since everything probably affects everything else, how can we ever make sense of the social world? If we are weighed down by that worry, though, we won't ever make progress. Every discipline that I am familiar with draws caricatures of the world in order to make sense of it. The modern economist does this by building *models*, which are deliberately stripped down representations of the phenomena out there. When I say "stripped down," I really mean stripped down. It isn't uncommon among us economists to focus on one or two causal factors, exclude everything else, hoping that this will enable us to understand how just those aspects of reality work and interact. The economist John Maynard Keynes described our subject thus: "Economics is a science of thinking in terms of models joined to the art of choosing models which are relevant to the contemporary world."

Influential economist John Maynard Keynes (right) meets with Harry Dexter White, Assistant Secretary to the Treasury, in 1946.

As economists deal with quantifiable objects (calories consumed, hours worked, tons of steel produced, miles of cable laid, square miles of equatorial forests destroyed), the models are almost always mathematical constructs. They can be stated in words, but mathematics is an enormously efficient way to express the structure of a model; more interestingly, for discovering the implications of a model. Applied mathematicians and physicists have known this for a long time, but it was only in the second half of the twentieth century that economists brazenly adopted that research tactic; as have related disciplines, such as ecology. The art of good modeling is to generate a lot of understanding from focusing on a very small number of causal factors. I say "art," because there is no formula for creating a good model. The acid test of a model is whether it discriminates among alternative explanations of a phenomenon. Those that survive empirical tests are accepted—at least for a while—until further evidence comes along that casts doubt on them, in which case economists go back to their drawing board to create better (not necessarily bigger!) models. And so on.

The methodology I have sketched here, all too briefly, enables economists to make a type of prediction that doesn't involve forecasting the future, but instead to make predictions of what the data that haven't yet been collected from the contemporary world will reveal. This is risky business, but if a model is to illuminate, it had better do more than just offer explanations after the events.

Until recently, economists studied economic history in much the same way historians study social and political history. They tried to uncover reasons why events in a particular place unfolded in the way they did, by identifying what they believed to be the key drivers there. The stress was on the uniqueness of the events being studied. A classic research topic in that mold involved asking why the first industrial revolution occurred in the eighteenth century and why it took place in England. As you can see, the question was based on three presumptions: there *was* a first industrial revolution; it occurred in the eighteenth century; and it was based in England. All three premises have been questioned, of course, but there was an enormous amount of work to be done even among those who had arrived at those premises from historical study. In the event, the literature built round those questions is one of the great achievements of economic history.

In recent years economists have added to that a statistical approach to the study of the past. The new approach stays close to economic

Nineteenth-century artist Phillip Jakob Louterbourg painted *Coalbrookdale by Night*, depicting an English Industrial Revolution scene, as blast furnaces light up the night in Coalbrookdale, an iron-making town.

theory, by laying emphasis on the generality of the processes that shape events. It adopts the view that a theory should uncover those features that are common among economic pathways in different places, at different times. Admittedly, no two economies are the same, but modern economists work on the commonality in the human experience, not so much on its differences. Say you want to identify the contemporary features in Desta's and Becky's worlds that best explain why the standard of living in the former is so much lower than in the latter. A body of economic models tells you that those features are represented by the variables X, Y, and Z. You look up international statistics on X, Y, and Z from a sample of, perhaps, 149 countries. The figures differ from country to country, but you regard the variables themselves as the explanatory factors common to all the countries in the sample. In other words, you interpret the 149 countries as parallel economies; and you treat features that are unique to each country as idiosyncrasies of that country. Of course, you aren't quite at liberty to model those idiosyncrasies any way you like. Statistical theory—which in the present context is called *econometrics*—will set limits on the way you are able to model them.

On the basis of the data on the 149 countries in your sample, you can now test whether you should be confident that X, Y, and Z are the factors determining the standard of living. Suppose the tests inform you that you are entitled to be confident. Then further analysis with the data will also enable you to determine how much of the variation in the standard of living in the sample is explained by variations in X in the sample, by variations in Y, and by variations in Z. Those proportions will give you a sense of the relative importance of the factors that determine the standard of living. Suppose 80% of the variation in the standard of living in those 149 countries can be explained by the variation in X in the sample; the remaining 20% by variations in Y and Z. You wouldn't be unjustified to conclude, tentatively, that X is the prime explanatory variable.

There are enormous problems in applying statistics to economic data. For example, it may be that your economic models, taken together, suggest that there could be as many as, say, 67 factors determining the standard of living (not just X, Y, and Z). However, you have a sample of only 149 countries. Any statistician will now tell you that 149 is too small a number for the task of unraveling the role of 67 factors. And there are other problems besetting the econometrician. But before you abandon statistics and rush back to the narrative style of empirical discourse, ask yourself why anyone should believe one scholar's historical narrative over another's. You may even wonder whether the scholar's literary flair may have influenced your appreciation of her work. Someone now reassures you that even the author of a historical narrative has a model in mind. He tells you that the author's model influenced her choice of the evidence displayed in her work, that she chose as she did only after having sifted through a great deal of evidence. You ask in response how you are to judge whether her conceptual model is better than someone else's. Which brings us back to the problem of testing alternative models of social phenomena. In the next chapter we will discover that historical narratives continue to play an important role in modern economics, but they are put to work in conjunction with model-building and econometric tests.

There are implicit assumptions underlying econometric tests that are hard to evaluate (how the country-specific idiosyncrasies are modeled is only one of them). So, economic statistics are often at

M.I.T. professor Robert Solow's groundbreaking studies of economic growth include the influential Solow model of growth theory. Such macroeconomic models are employed to study and predict economic developments.

best translucent. It isn't uncommon for several competing models to coexist, each having its own champion. Model-building, data availability, historical narratives, and advances in econometric techniques reinforce one other. As the economist Robert Solow expresses it, "facts ask for explanations, and explanations ask for new facts."

In this monograph, I first want to give you a feel for the way we economists go about uncovering the economic pathways that shape Becky's and Desta's lives. I shall do that by addressing the three sorts of questions that were identified earlier as our concern. I shall then explain why we need economic policies and how we should go about identifying good ones. We will certainly build models as we go along, but I shall mostly use words to describe them. I shall also refer to empirical findings, from anthropology, demography, ecology, geography, political science, sociology, and of course economics itself. But the lens through which we will study the social world is that of *economics*. We will assume a point of view of the circumstances of living that gives prominence to the allocation of scarce resources—among contemporaries and across the generations. My idea is to take you on a tour to see how far we are able to reach an understanding of the social world around us and beyond.

ONE

Macroeconomic History

•

I SAID ONE OF THE THINGS WE need to do if we are to understand Becky's and Desta's lives is to uncover the pathways by which their families came to inherit their current circumstances. This is the stuff of economic history. In studying history, we could, should we feel bold, take the long view—from about the time agriculture came to be settled practice in the northern part of the Fertile Crescent (roughly, southeast Turkey today) some 11,000 years ago—and try to explain why the many innovations and practices that have cumulatively contributed to the making of Becky's world either didn't reach or didn't take hold in Desta's part of the world.

Scholars have tried to do that. The geographer Jared Diamond, for example, has argued that people in the super-continent of Eurasia have

A NASA satellite image of Iraq shows the Tigris (right) and Euphrates (left) rivers, between which lies Mesopotamia's Fertile Crescent, where many advanced agricultural practices and innovations originated.

enjoyed two potent sets of advantages over people elsewhere. First, unlike Africa and the Americas, Eurasia is oriented along an east–west axis in the temperate zone and contains no overpowering mountain range or desert to prevent the diffusion of people, ideas, seeds, and animals. Second, Eurasia was blessed with a large number of domesticatable species of animals, which made it possible for humans there to engage in tasks they wouldn't have been able to undertake on their own. Economies grew and declined in different parts of Eurasia at different times—now India, now China, now Persia, now Islam, now one region in Europe, then another—but the super-continent's size and orientation meant that, during the past 11,000 years, humanity's achievements there have been rather like the performance of financial stocks: declines in some regions have been matched by growth in others. By the 16th century, the technological gap between the seafaring nations of Western Europe and the Americas was so large that a combination of guns, steel, and European germs enabled tiny groups of invaders to conquer the New World. Becky's very successful part of the world is in effect the outgrowth of a societal transplant that took place less than 500 years ago.

GDP as Measuring Rod

In order to talk of success and failure, as we are doing here, we need a measuring rod. The one most commonly used today is *gross domestic product* per person, or *GDP* per capita. Economists may have invented the concept and may have also warned against its many limitations; but, like it or not, the term is so ingrained in public consciousness, that if someone exclaims, "Economic growth!", we don't need to ask, "Growth in what?"—we know they mean growth in *real* GDP per capita; which is growth in GDP per capita, corrected for inflation or deflation.

A country's GDP is the value of all the final goods that are produced by its residents in a given year. It is a measure of an economy's total output. But when a commodity is produced and sold, the price paid for the purchase finds its way into someone's pocket. So, GDP can be measured also by adding up everyone's incomes—wages, salaries, interests, profits, and government income. GDP and national income are therefore two sides of the same coin.

Although GDP is often said to measure wealth, it doesn't do so. GDP is a flow (dollars per year, say), whereas wealth is a stock (dollars—period). As the concept of GDP was developed originally for market economies, the values imputed to the goods were market prices. But by a clever construction of notional prices (called "shadow prices"; Chapters 7–8), economists have adapted GDP even for economies like Desta's, where much economic activity is undertaken in non-market institutions. It was by imputing values to the produce taken from the local commons in Desta's village that economic statisticians concluded that one-fifth of her household's income amounts to the value of goods obtained directly from the natural resources in her locality, a figure I reported when describing Desta's world.

Adjusting for differences in the cost of living across the world, global income per head today is about $8,000 a year. But for most of humanity's past, people have been abysmally poor. The economic statistician Angus Maddison has estimated from the very fragmentary evidence that exists, that, at the beginning of our Common Era (0 CE) the per capita income of the world was about $515 a year in today's prices. If Maddison's estimate is even approximately correct, it means that the average person 2,000 years ago enjoyed not much more than a dollar a day, a figure deemed by the World Bank as the line below which a person is in extreme poverty.

Maddison has also suggested that the distribution of income 2,000 years ago was remarkably equal: almost everyone, everywhere was very poor. The figures he has reported tell us furthermore that average world income and the regional distribution of income per head were pretty much the same in 1000 CE as they had been 1,000 years earlier. It would appear that regional disparities became significant only from the beginning of the nineteenth century: income per head in Western Europe had by then become three times that in Africa. But world income per head was still only $755 a year in today's prices, meaning that it had increased by less than 50% over a 1,800-year period; amounting to an annual growth rate of under 0.02%. The figure is extremely low by contemporary standards: the annual growth rate of income per head has been about 2% a year over the past four decades. (A useful formula to remember is that, if a numerical entity—say real GDP per person—grows (or declines) at the annual rate of g%, that entity doubles (or halves) approximately every $70/g$ years. Examples: GDP per capita would double every 35 years if it were to grow at an annual rate of 2%; and halve every 140 years if it declined at an annual rate of 0.5%.)

Large regional disparities in income are also less than 200 years old. The ratio of the average incomes in the US and Africa has risen from 3 at the beginning of the nineteenth century to more than 20 today—about $38,000 compared to $1,850 per year. Real GDP per capita in the US has grown 30 times in size in 200 years, implying that the average annual growth rate of income per person there has been about 1.7%. In sad contrast, income per capita in Ethiopia is about the same today as it was 200 years ago (a little over $700 a year today), a fact that is reflected in the differences we noted between the incomes per member in Becky's and Desta's households, respectively.

The World Bank's stated goal is the reduction of poverty in developing countries.

If you were to line up countries according to GDP per capita today, you would find two clusters: one poor (Desta's world), the other rich (Becky's world). There are middle-income nations spread thinly between the extremes (China, Brazil, Venezuela, and Argentina are prominent examples), but a large cluster of countries (in sub-Saharan Africa, the Indian subcontinent, South East Asia, Melanesia, and Central America)—with a total population of 2.3 billion—produces an average $2,100 a year per head, while another, smaller, cluster (Europe, North America, Australia, and Japan)—with a total population of a little under 1 billion—enjoys an average annual income of $30,000 (see Table 1 on page 24). The world would appear to be polarized. Moreover, with the possible exception of India, there is little sign that the poor world will catch up with the rich world in the foreseeable future. During the past four decades, real per capita GDP has grown at an average annual rate of 2.4% in rich countries, whereas it has grown at 1.8% in poor countries (Table 1). Worse, within the poor world, sub-Saharan Africa has experienced a small decline in real GDP per capita during the past four decades.

In contrast to poor countries, agricultural output is a small fraction of national income in the rich world. The share of agriculture in GDP is about 25% in the poor world; less than 5% in rich countries. Less than 10% of the population in rich countries live in rural areas. In contrast, more than 70% of people in poor countries live in villages (Table 1); which gives rise to the thought that people in poor countries mostly work in economies that draw their production inputs directly from Nature—they are "biomass-based" economies. Ecology is of direct concern to the world's poor, in a way it isn't to the world's rich.

Recently, the United Nations Development Programme (UNDP) has sought to extend the basis on which the standard of living is measured. It has done so by constructing a numerical index that combines GDP per capita, life expectancy at birth, and literacy. UNDP has christened it the Human Development Index (HDI). Again, leaving aside a few exceptions, HDI has been found to be low in poor countries, high in rich countries (Table 1).

Proximate Causes behind Differences between Becky's and Desta's Worlds

What enables people in Becky's world to be so much richer than people in Desta's world? Several features suggest themselves.

People in rich countries have better equipment to work with (electric drills are more powerful than pickaxes; tractors are superior to plows; and modern medicine is vastly more effective than traditional cures). So, one argument goes that the accumulation of physical capital (more accurately, *manufactured* capital) in Becky's world has been a significant contributor to the high standard of living people enjoy there. This could be the factor *X* that I mentioned in the Prologue to illustrate the way economic theory and applied economics mesh today.

Others have noted that people in rich countries are far better educated, implying that they are able to make use of ideas to produce goods that are out of reach for people in countries where large numbers are illiterate. A crude index of education is the proportion of adults (people aged 15 and above) who are literate, the figure for which today is over 95% in the rich world, but only 58% in the poor world (Table 1). Gender inequalities are considerably greater in the poor than in the rich world. The proportion of adult women who are literate in poor countries is 48%, whereas in the rich world the corresponding proportion is pretty much the same as that for men, namely, over 95% (Table 1). Allied to education is health. Life expectancy at birth in rich countries is now 78 years, whereas it is about 58 years in poor countries. Some 120 children among every 1,000 of those under 5 years of age die each year in the poor world; the corresponding figure for rich countries is 7 (Table 1).

	Rich nations	Poor nations
Population (billions)	1.0	2.3
GDP per capita	$30,000	$2,100
Human Development Index	high	low
Annual population growth rate (%): 1966–2004	0.8	2.4
Annual growth rate of GDP per capita (%): 1966–2004	2.4	1.8
Total fertility rate (TFR)	1.8	3.7
Adult literacy (%) (female literacy (%))	>95 (>95)	58 (48)
Index of government corruption	low	high
Life expectancy at birth (years)	78	58
Under 5 mortality (per 1,000)	7	120
Rural popuation (% of total population)	10	70
Agriculture's share in GDP (%)	5	25

Source: *World Development Indicators* (World Bank, 2005)

Table 1. Rich and poor nations

Clean water and good hygiene have also reduced morbidity in rich countries greatly. About one-quarter of the population in the poor world suffer from undernourishment, whereas the corresponding figure in rich countries is negligible. As malnutrition and vulnerability to infections reinforce each other, poor nourishment and morbidity go together.

There is evidence that undernourishment in early childhood affects the development of cognitive faculties. Taken together, the average person in the rich world is capable of supplying work of far higher quality and for many more years than his counterpart in a poor country. Education and health go by the name *human capital*. A literature pioneered by the economists Theodore Schultz and Gary Becker reveals that the accumulation of human capital has been a significant factor behind the high standard of living people in Becky's world enjoy today. This could be the factor Y that was mentioned in the Prologue.

Many economists, however, regard the production of new ideas as the prime factor behind economic progress. They say that rich countries have become rich because people there have been successful in producing ideas not only for new products (printing press, steam engine, electricity, chemical products, the electronic computer), but also for cheaper ways of

The people of wealthy nations have long had access to superior technologies. An 1874 Currier & Ives lithograph depicts two "lightning express" trains departing the station.

producing old products (transportation, mining). Of course, education and advances in science and technology combine as an economic force. Primary and secondary education alone can't take a society that far today. A country where tertiary education is low would not have a population capable of working with the most advanced technology. Nor are scientific and technological advances capable of being achieved today by people with no advanced education. Ideas could be the factor Z that was mentioned in the Prologue.

Related to this is an issue that has proved to be far more contentious than it should have been: population growth. Even unaided intuition suggests that if numbers grow quickly, the rate at which capital assets must increase would need to be high in order to maintain living standards. If the desire to accumulate physical and human capital is the same in two countries, and if rising numbers don't reduce the cost of accumulating that capital, the country where population grows at a slower rate can be expected to enjoy a higher living standard in the long run. Since the mid-1960s, population in what is today the poor world has grown at an average annual rate of about 2.4%, while the corresponding figure in today's rich world has been about 0.8% (Table 1). This is a big difference. Statistical demographers now agree that, controlling for other factors, countries where population increase has been large in recent decades have experienced slow growth in real GDP per capita. Later in this book we will note that high population growth in today's poor countries has also put enormous pressure on their ecology, creating further problems for rural people.

A country's population growth is affected not just by net reproduction, but by net immigration and the age distribution too. In order to isolate net reproduction, it is common practice to work with the *fertility rate* (more accurately, the *total fertility rate* or *TFR*), which is the number of live births a woman expects to deliver over her life. Suppose parents desire to have a certain number of surviving children. Then the fertility rate should decline once the mortality rate among children under five starts to decline. Demographers have puzzled why reductions in fertility rates in today's poor world have been slower than they had expected. The first known decline in fertility rates in northwestern Europe (England and France especially) occurred in the seventeenth century, when the rate fell from about 7 to 4 (See Chapter 6). The fertility rate in the rich world today is 1.8 (below 2.1, the figure at which population would stabilize in the long run), whereas it is 3.7 in the poor world (Table 1). Despite a significant decline in child mortality rates, the TFR in a number of countries in sub-Saharan Africa continues to be between 6 and 8. We should ask whether there have been countervailing forces at work to keep fertility rates high in that continent. We should ask too whether the resulting population growth has been a factor in its terrible economic performance over the past four decades. We will study the question in greater detail in Chapter 6, but one implication of high fertility rates for women's conditions follows at once.

In sub-Saharan Africa, extended breastfeeding has been a traditional practice for controlling pregnancies. Among the !Kung San nomads of the Kalahari Desert, children have been known to be breastfed until they are 4 years old. Even if we were to ignore such extreme cases, successful reproduction in Africa would involve two years of pregnancy and breastfeeding. This means that in societies where female life expectancy at birth is greater than 45 years and the fertility rate is 8, girls can expect to spend more than half their fecund life (say, 15–45) in pregnancy or nursing; and we have not allowed for unsuccessful pregnancies. Under these circumstances, women such as Desta's mother are unable ever to seek employment outside subsistence agriculture.

With a child strapped to her waist, a woman gathers berries in Kalahari Desert, Namibia.

No economist has ever claimed that there is a single driving force behind economic growth. All would appear to agree that the accumulation of manufactured capital, human capital, and the production, diffusion, and use of new scientific and technological ideas go together, each contributing positively to the contributions of the others. In the contemporary world, an accumulation of, say, manufactured capital goods raises real GDP, other things being equal. This enables societies to set aside more of their incomes for education and health, triggering a reduction in both fertility and child mortality. Education increases GDP further, other things being equal, while reduced fertility and child mortality typically lower population growth; which, taken together, enable societies to set aside more of their incomes for the production of new ideas. This raises the productivity of manufactured capital; which in turn brings forth further accumulation of manufactured capital; and so on, in a virtuous cycle of prosperity. The flip side of this is, of course, a vicious cycle of poverty. The polarization that separates the rich and poor worlds today is a manifestation of those two movements. Economists use the terms *virtuous* and *vicious* cycles to characterize polarization (a few of us refer to vicious cycles as *poverty traps*); mathematicians say instead that the poor and rich worlds are in two different *basins of attraction*.

It is possible to discover the relative importance of the various factors responsible for economic growth. No doubt the answer is different in different places and in different periods of history; but five decades ago, Robert Solow showed us how to investigate the question, by devising a way to decompose recorded changes in an economy's real GDP into their measurable sources. In contrast to the empirical exercise on *cross* country statistics that I described in the Prologue, the idea here is to measure *changes* in *X, Y, Z* over a period of time in a given country and estimate the relative importance of those changes for growth in real GDP there over that same period. Suppose that over an interval of time a country's real GDP has increased. Solow, and subsequently others, showed how to attribute that growth to increases in labor force participation (population growth; increases in women's employment in paid labor), the accumulation of human skills and manufactured capital, improvements in the quality of machinery and equipment, and so on. Now suppose that when we have added up all the contributions made by these factors of production, we find that the sum falls short of real GDP growth. We are entitled then to interpret that shortfall as an increase in the overall productivity of the economy's capital assets; by which we mean that more output can be produced now than earlier, even if the amounts of such factors of production as machines and equipment and skills had remained the same. This is a formal way of acknowledging that there has been a general rise in the efficiency with which goods are produced. Economists call that rise growth in *total factor productivity*.

Growth of *total factor productivity* is defined by an increase in the efficiency with which goods are produced. Workers building a Model T in the early twentieth century are on an assembly line, the development of which allowed Ford Motor Company to mass-produce the automobile.

How does that latter growth come about? It comes about when people acquire knowledge and make use of it, or when people make better use of what they already know. Which is why economists often refer to growth in total factor productivity as *technological progress*. But there are other changes in an economy that could leave an imprint on total factor productivity, such as improvements in the workings of institutions. Growth in total factor productivity may be an ungainly way to convey an idea, but it reflects the unexplained bit of real GDP growth pretty well. In the economics literature the name has come to stay.

Since World War II, growth in total factor productivity in the rich world has been considerable. It has been estimated, for example, that during 1970–2000 the average annual rate of growth of total factor productivity in the United Kingdom (UK) was 0.7%. Economists have estimated that, in contrast, total factor productivity *declined* slightly in a number of countries in sub-Saharan Africa during that same period.

What do these figures mean? Take the case of the UK. The country's real GDP grew at an average annual rate of 2.4%, which means about 29% of that growth (that is, 0.7/2.4) could be attributed to increases in total factor productivity. At 2.4% growth rate, real GDP in year 2000 was twice the real GDP in 1970. Nearly one-third of that increase can be attributed to growth in total factor productivity. In contrast, the economies in sub-Saharan Africa where total factor productivity declined during that period became less efficient in their use of such factors of production as machines and equipment, skills and labor hours. It's hard to believe that people in those countries systematically forgot technical knowledge they had known in the past. So the decline in total factor productivity there must have been due to a deterioration in local institutions, precipitated by civil wars and bad governance.

These statistics raise a puzzle. Today's poor countries lie mainly in the tropics, whereas the rich countries are mostly in temperate zones. No doubt the tropics are a breeding ground for many diseases, but they also harbor vast quantities of natural resources (timber; minerals; and conditions suitable for the production of spices, fibers, coffee, and tea). During the past several centuries, the countries that are rich today have been importing those very resources and products to fuel their factories and mills, and to make their meals enjoyable. They accumulated machines, human capital, and also produced scientific and technological knowledge. Why didn't the poor world take advantage of their resource endowments to enrich themselves in the same way?

Colonization is a possible answer. Historians have shown that, from the sixteenth century, European powers have extracted natural resources from the colonies—including cheap (read, slave) labor—but

A seventeenth-century French engraving depicts West Indian slaves manufacturing sugar. Many advanced nations considered slaves to be just another natural resource to be extracted from their colonies.

have mostly invested the proceeds domestically. Of course, one should ask why it is that the Europeans managed to colonize the tropics; why colonization didn't take place the other way around. As noted earlier, Jared Diamond has offered an answer. That said, many of the most prominent of those ex-colonies have been politically independent for decades now. During that time real income per head in the rich world has increased over and over again. With the exception of a few striking examples in South and South East Asia, though, most of the ex-colonies have either remained poor or become poorer still. Why?

Institutions

Economic historians such as Robert Fogel, David Landes, and Douglass North have argued that the rich world is rich today because, over the centuries, it has devised institutions that have enabled people to improve their material conditions of life. This is a deeper explanation. It says that people in rich countries work with superior technologies, are healthier, live longer, are better educated, and produce many more productive ideas, *because* they have been able to get on with their lives in societies whose institutions permit—even encourage—the economy-wide accumulation of such factors of production as machines, transport facilities, health, skills, ideas, and the fruits of those ideas. The accumulation of productive capital assets is only a proximate cause of prosperity, the real cause is progressive institutions.

One can peel away the conceptual onion some more, and ask how and why past people in today's rich countries were able to fashion their institutions in ways that enabled those proximate causes of prosperity to explode there. One can even ask whether institutions did it, or whether it was the enlightened policies of the rulers that were responsible for the explosion.

But then, policies aren't plucked from air, they emerge from consultations and deliberations within institutions. Nor is it likely that a policy designed to bring prosperity to a country will actually work unless the institutions there are capable of implementing it.

These dilemmas are of enormous importance for today's poor countries. What institutions should they adopt and what policies should their governments be encouraged to follow? There is little point in embarking on grandiose projects (steel mills, petrochemical plants, land reform, public health programs, free education) unless a country's institutions have the necessary checks and balances to limit corruption and wastage. This brings us back to our earlier question: how did those institutions that promoted economic growth in today's rich countries become established and flourish? Despite the attention the question has received from the world's most outstanding economic historians, the matter remains unsettled. In the next chapter I shall show why it is inherently so difficult to find a satisfactory answer (which, I guess, is itself a mark of increased understanding). In view of the difficulties, it is safest to regard institutions as the explanatory factor when we seek to understand why Becky's and Desta's worlds differ so much in terms of the standard of living.

The Oxford English Dictionary defines *institution* as "an established law, custom, usage, practice, organization, or other element in the political or social life of a people." We shall follow that lead, but recast it so as to stress the role of institutions in economic life. By institutions I shall mean, very loosely, the *arrangements* that govern collective undertakings. Those arrangements include not only legal entities, like the firm where Becky's father works, but also the *iddir* to which Desta's father belongs. They include the markets in which Becky's family purchase goods and services, and the rural networks Desta's household belongs to. They include the nuclear household in Becky's world and the extended kinship system of claims and obligations in Desta's world. And they include that overarching entity called *government* in both their worlds.

Institutions are defined in part by the rules and authority structure that govern collective undertakings, but in part also by the relationships they have with outsiders. The rules on the factory floor (who is expected to do which task, who has authority over whom, and so on) matter not only to members of the firm, they matter to others too. For example, rich countries have laws relating to working conditions in factories. Moreover, environmental regulations constrain what firms are able to do with their effluents. In every society there are layers of rules of varied coverage. Some rules come under other rules, many have legal force, while others are at best tacit understandings.

Poverty-stricken nations often look to land-reform projects to improve public welfare. Such programs, however, often result in persecution and corruption. A Zimbabwean farmer (left) meets with a political official and journalists in 2009 to discuss occupation of his land by proponents of Zimbabwe's controversial land-reform program.

The effectiveness of an institution depends on the rules governing it and on whether its members obey the rules. The codes of conduct in the civil service of every country include honesty, but governments differ enormously as to its practice. Social scientists have constructed indices of corruption among public officials. One such index is based on the perception private firms have acquired, on the basis of their experience, of the bribes people have had to pay officials in order to do business. The index (see Table 1)—which is on a scale of 1 (highly corrupt) to 10 (highly clean)— is less than 3.5 for most poor countries (African countries and Eastern Europe are among the worst) and greater than 7 for most rich countries (Scandinavian countries are among the best). It used to be argued that bribery of public officials helps to raise national income because it lubricates economic transactions. It does so in a corrupt world: if you don't pay up, you don't get to do business. But corruption isn't an inevitable evil. There are several poor countries where corruption is low. Having to pay bribes raises production costs; so less is produced. Citizens suffer, because the price they have to pay for products is that much higher.

Economists have speculated that government corruption is related to the delays people face in having the rule of law enforced. The thought is that delays are a way of eliciting bribes to hasten legal processes. To enforce a contract takes 415 days in the poor world, as against 280 days in the rich world. It may be that corruption is also related to government ineffectiveness. To register a business takes 66 days in the poor world, 27 days in the rich world. In poor countries, registering property takes 100 days on average, while in rich countries the figure is 50 days. Some economists have suggested that government officials in poor countries create lengthy waits (that's government ineffectiveness) so as to elicit bribes from applicants if they want to jump those lines (that's corruption).

Most Ethiopians, living from subsistence farming, make little use of currency such as this one *birr* banknote, yet money is necessary when dealing with corrupt government officials who demand bribes.

How do government corruption, ineffectiveness, and indifference to the rule of law translate into the kind of macroeconomic statistics we have been studying here? They leave their imprint on total factor productivity. Other things being equal, a country whose government is corrupt or ineffective, or where the rule of law is not respected, is a country whose total factor productivity is lower than that of a country whose government suffers from fewer of those defects. Some scholars call these intangible but quantifiable factors *social infrastructure*, others call them *social capital*.

Institutions are overarching entities. People interact with one another *in* institutions. A more basic notion is that of *engagements* among people. The possibility of engagements gives rise to a fundamental problem in economic life. We study that next.

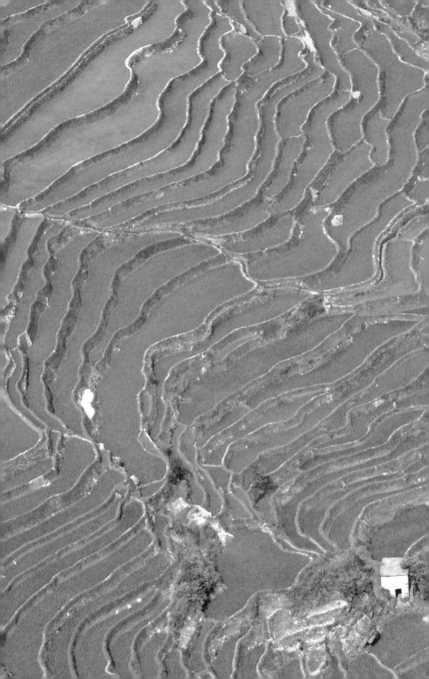

TWO

Trust

●

IMAGINE THAT A GROUP OF PEOPLE have discovered a mutually advantageous course of actions. At the grandest level, it could be that citizens see the benefits of adopting a constitution for their country. At a more local level, the undertaking could be to share the costs and benefits of maintaining a communal resource (irrigation system, grazing field, coastal fishery); construct a jointly useable asset (drainage channel in a watershed); collaborate in political activity (civic engagement, lobbying); do business when the purchase and delivery of goods can't be synchronized (credit, insurance, wage labor); enter marriage; create a rotating saving and credit association (*iddir*); initiate a reciprocal arrangement (I help you, now that you are in need, with the understanding that you will help me when I am in need); adopt a convention (send one another Christmas cards); create a partnership to produce goods for the market;

These rice-paddy terraces in Yunnan province, China, are a communal resource, essential to the irrigation and cultivation of the region's staple crop.

enter into an instantaneous transaction (purchase something across the counter); and so on. Then there are mutually advantageous courses of action that involve being civil to one another. They range from such forms of civic behavior as not disfiguring public spaces and obeying the law more generally, to respecting the rights of others.

Imagine next that the parties have agreed to share the benefits and costs in a certain way. Again, at the grandest level the agreement could be a social contract among citizens to observe their constitution. Or it could be a tacit agreement to be civil to one another, such as respecting the rights of others to be heard, to get on with their lives, and so forth. Here we will be thinking of agreements over transactions in goods and services. There would be situations where the agreement was based on a take-it-or-leave-it offer one party made to another (as when Becky's mother accepts the terms and conditions set by the firm called in by her to fix the plumbing). In other contexts, bargaining may have been involved (as when Desta's mother purchases household fineries at the regional fair, which is not altogether different from a Middle Eastern bazaar). Later in this book (Chapter 4) we will study an idealized version of prices in the markets Becky's family visits, where both buyers and sellers face take-it-or-leave-it offers. But we will not study how agreements are reached when bargaining is involved in either Becky's or Desta's worlds, nor look for principles of equity that might have been invoked during negotiation. To do that would take us into bargaining theory, a beautiful but difficult branch of the theory of games. We ask instead a question that is pertinent in both Becky's and Desta's worlds: *Under what circumstances would the parties who have reached agreement trust one another to keep their word?*

Because one's word must be credible if it is to be believed, mere promises wouldn't be enough. (Witness that we warn others—and ourselves too—not to trust people "blindly.") If the parties are to trust one another to keep their promise, matters must be so arranged that: (1) at every stage of the agreed course of actions, it would be in the interest of each party to plan to keep his or her word if all others were to plan to keep their word; and (2) at every stage of the agreed course of actions, each party would believe that all others would keep their word. If the two conditions are met, a system of beliefs that the agreement will be kept would be self-confirming.

Notice that condition (2) on its own wouldn't do. Beliefs need to be justified. Condition (1) provides the justification. It offers the basis on which everyone could in principle believe that the agreement will be kept. A course of actions, one per party, satisfying condition (1) is

Princeton mathematician John Forbes Nash Jr. is the founder of modern game theory, which has become essential to the study of economic behavior.

called a *Nash equilibrium*, in honor of the mathematician John Nash— he of *A Beautiful Mind*—who proved that it is not a vacuous concept. (Nash showed that the condition can be met in realistic situations.) The way I have stated condition (1) isn't due to Nash, though, but to John Harsanyi, Thomas Schelling, and Reinhard Selten, three social scientists who refined the concept of Nash equilibrium so that it could be applied to situations where Nash's own formulation is not adequate.

Notice that condition (1) on its own wouldn't do either. It could be that it is in each one's interest to behave opportunistically if everyone believed that everyone else would behave opportunistically. In that case non-cooperation is also a Nash equilibrium, meaning that a set of mutual beliefs that the agreement will not be kept would also be self-confirming. Stated somewhat informally, a Nash equilibrium is a course of actions (*strategy*, in economic parlance) per party, such that no party would have any reason to deviate from his or her course of actions if all other parties were to pursue their courses of actions. As a general rule, societies harbor more than one Nash equilibrium. Some yield desirable outcomes, others do not. The fundamental problem every society faces is to create institutions where conditions (1) and (2) apply to engagements that protect and promote its members' interests. When we come to study what economics has to say about the ideal role of the state (Chapter 8), we will have much to add about those interests.

Conditions (1) and (2), taken together, require an awful lot of coordination among the parties. In order to probe the question of which Nash equilibrium can be expected to be reached—if a Nash equilibrium is expected to be reached at all—economists study human behavior that are *not* Nash equilibria. The idea is to model the way people form beliefs about the way the world works, the way people behave, and the way they revise their beliefs on the basis of what they observe. The idea is to track the consequences of those patterns of belief formation so as to check whether the model moves toward a Nash equilibrium over time, or whether it moves about in some fashion or other but not toward an equilibrium.

This research enterprise has yielded a general conclusion. Suppose the economic environment in a certain place harbors more than one Nash equilibrium. Which equilibrium should be expected to be approached—if the economy approaches an equilibrium at all—will depend on the beliefs that people held at some point in the past. It also depends on the way people have revised their beliefs on the basis of observations since that past date. But this is another way of saying that history matters. The narrative style of empirical economics that I spoke of earlier becomes necessary at this point. Model-building, statistical tests on data relating to the models, and historical narratives have to work together synergistically if we are to make progress in understanding our social world. Unfortunately, the study of disequilibrium behavior would lengthen this monograph greatly. So I shall only allude to it from time to time. We will discover that, fortunately, a study of equilibrium behavior takes us a long way.

We started this chapter by observing that mutual trust is the basis of cooperation. In view of what we have learned about the multiplicity of Nash equilibria, we are now led to ask what kinds of institution are capable of supporting cooperation. To answer that, it will prove useful to classify the contexts in which the promises people make to one another are credible.

Mutual Affection

Consider the situation where the people involved care about one another and it is commonly known that they care about one another. The household is the most obvious example of an institution based on affection. To break a promise we have made to someone we care about is to feel bad. So we try not to do it. From time to time, though, even household members are tempted to misbehave. As people who live together can observe one another closely, the risk of being caught misbehaving is high. This restrains household members even when the temptation to misbehave is great.

That said, the household can't engage in enterprises that require people of many and varied talents. So households need to find ways to do business with others. The problem of trust reappears at the interhousehold level. This leads us to search for other contexts in which people can trust one another to keep their word.

Pro-social Disposition

One such situation is where people are trustworthy, or where they reciprocate if others have behaved well toward them. Evolutionary psychologists have suggested that we are adapted to have a general disposition to reciprocate. Development psychologists have found that pro-social disposition can be formed by communal living, role-modeling, education, and receiving rewards and punishments (be it here or in the afterlife).

We don't have to choose between the two viewpoints; they are not mutually exclusive. Our capacity to have such feelings as shame, guilt, fear, affection, anger, elation, reciprocity, benevolence, jealousy, and our sense of fairness and justice have emerged under selection pressure. Culture helps to shape preferences, expectations, and our notion of what constitutes fairness. Those in turn influence behavior, which are known to differ among societies. But cultural coordinates enable us to identify the situations *in* which shame, guilt, fear, affection, anger, elation, reciprocity, benevolence, and jealousy arise; they don't displace the centrality of those feelings in the human makeup. The thought I am exploring here is that, as adults, we not only have a disposition for such behavior as paying our dues, helping others at some cost to ourselves, and returning a favor, we also ease our hurt by punishing people who have hurt us intentionally; and shun people who break agreements, frown on those who socialize with people who have broken agreements, and so on. By internalizing norms of behavior, a person enables the springs of his actions to include them. In short, he has a disposition to obey the norm, be it personal or social. When he does violate it, neither guilt nor shame would typically be absent, but frequently the act will have been rationalized by him. Making a promise is a commitment for that person; and it is essential for him that others recognize it to be so.

People are trustworthy to varying degrees. When we refrain from breaking the law, it isn't always because of a fear of being caught. The problem is that although pro-social disposition isn't foreign to human nature, no society could rely exclusively on it. How is one to tell to what extent someone is trustworthy? If the personal benefits from betraying one's conscience are large enough, almost all of us would betray it. Most people have a price, but it's hard to tell who comes at what price.

Societies everywhere have tried to establish institutions where people have the incentives to do business with one another. The incentives differ in their details, but they have one thing in common: *those who break agreements without cause are punished*. Let us see how that is achieved.

Laws and Norms

There are two ways. One is to rely on an external enforcer, the other on mutual enforcement. Each gives rise to a particular type of institution. Depending on the nature of the business they would like to enter into, people invoke one or the other. The coded term for one is the *rule of law*; for the other, it is *social norm*. People in the rich world rely heavily on the former, while in the poor world people depend greatly on the latter. Subsequently we will study the claim that it is *because* they have been able to depend extensively on the former for centuries that people in the rich world are now rich.

I shall illustrate the two methods of enforcement with the help of a numerical example of bilateral agreement. The numbers will allow us to draw insights without fuss. The example itself is based on the "putting-out system" of production, widely practiced in Europe in the seventeenth and eighteenth centuries and prevalent in poor countries today in the crafts. The system amounted to a patron–client relationship, but for our purposes here it can also be thought of as a partnership.

Imagine that person A owns some working capital (raw material, say), worth \$4,000 to him. A knows B, who has the skills to use that capital to produce goods worth \$8,000 in the market. A doesn't have those skills. However, A has access to the market, which B doesn't. A proposes to advance his capital to her, with the understanding that he will sell the goods once B produces them and share the proceeds with her. If B was not to work for A, she would use her time to produce goods for her home, worth \$2,000 to her. In order to get her to accept his offer, A proposes a sharing rule that is hallowed by their tradition: the \$8,000 would be used first to compensate both parties fully—\$4,000 for A (the amount A would enjoy from the best alternative use of his working capital, which economists call the working capital's *opportunity cost*) and \$2,000 for B (which is the opportunity cost of B's time and effort); the remaining \$2,000 would then be divided equally between the two. A would receive \$5,000 and B \$3,000. Each would gain \$1,000 from the arrangement.

B regards the proposal as fair, but is worried about one thing: why should she trust A not to renege on the agreement by keeping the entire \$8,000 for himself?

External Enforcement

Here is one possible way to ensure that B could trust A: the agreement is enforced by an established structure of power and authority. In many societies, tribal chieftains, village or clan elders, and warlords enforce agreements and rule on disputes. Here we imagine that the external enforcer is the state and that the agreement is drawn up as a legal contract. We include on this list the implicit "social contract" among citizens not to break the law. However, if contracts are to offer a viable means of doing things, breaches must be *verifiable*; otherwise, the external enforcer would have nothing to go by if asked to rule on it. To be sure, lawyers, like Becky's father, make a handsome living precisely because verification is fraught with difficulties. Rough estimates suggest that in the US, expenditure on the legal profession (lawyers, judges, investigators), on people who work in insurance (loss adjusters, insurance agents), and on those in law enforcement (the police) make up $245 billion a year, which is about 2% of the US's GDP; and I haven't included the defensive measures people take against possible litigations, burglary, and theft.

Pakistani tribal elders prepare to tie the traditional turban to the head of their new tribal chief, the grandson of the former chief, who was killed during clashes between tribesmen and government security forces. In many regions of Pakistan, tribal elders are more respected and influential than the government.

We leave aside the problems that arise in verifying breach of contract (but see Chapters 4–5) and note that if the punishment the state imposes for a violation is known to be severe relative to the temptation A faces to violate, A will be deterred from going that route. If B is aware of the force of that deterrence, she will trust A not to renege. And A will trust B not to renege, because he knows B doesn't fear that he will renege. In Becky's world, the rules governing transactions in the market place are embodied in the law of contracts. Becky's father's firm is a legal entity, as are the financial institutions through which he is able to accumulate his retirement pension, save for Becky's and Sam's education, and so on. He has an employment contract with his firm. The agreements he has reached with the saving and pension institutions are legal contracts. Even when someone in the family goes to the grocery store, the purchases (paid in cash or by card) involve the law, which provides protection for both parties (the grocer, in case the cash is counterfeit or the card is void; the purchaser, in case the product turns out on inspection to be substandard). Formal markets, from which people enter and exit when they need to or wish to, are able to function only because there is an elaborate legal structure that enforces the agreements known as "purchases" and "sales." Moreover, it is because Becky's family, the grocery store's owner, and the credit card company are confident that the government has the ability and willingness to enforce contracts that they do business together.

Given that enforcing contracts involves resources, what is the basis of that confidence? After all, the contemporary world has shown that there are states and there are states. One answer—in a functioning democracy—is that the government worries about its reputation. A free and inquisitive press helps to sober the government into believing that incompetence or corruption would mean an end to its rule, come the next election. Notice how this involves a system of interlocking beliefs about one another's abilities and intentions. The millions of households in Becky's country trust their government (more or less!) to enforce contracts, because they know that government leaders know that not to enforce contracts efficiently would mean being thrown out of office. In their turn, each side of a contract trusts the other not to renege (again, more or less!), because each knows that the other knows that the government can be trusted to enforce contracts. And so on. Trust is maintained by the threat of punishment (a fine, a jail term, dismissal, or whatever) for anyone who breaks a contract, be the contract legal (Becky's father's employment contract) or social (the contract between the voters and the government in Becky's world to maintain law and order). We are in the realm of beliefs that are held together by their own bootstraps (our earlier condition (2)).

What I have presented is only the sketch of an argument. The complete argument is similar to the one which shows that social norms also offer a way to enforce agreements. So I turn to that for details.

Mutual Enforcement

Although the law of contracts exists in Desta's country, her family can't depend on it. The nearest courts are far away and there are no lawyers in sight. As transport is very costly, her village is something of an enclave. Economic life is shaped outside a formal legal system. Nevertheless, Desta's parents do business with others. Saving for funerals involves saying, "I accept the terms and conditions of the *iddir*." As there are no formal credit markets where they live, villagers practice reciprocity so as to smooth consumption. A recent study has found that in a sample of villages in Nigeria nearly all credit transactions were either between relatives or between households in the same village. No written contracts were involved, nor did the agreements specify the date of repayment or the amount repaid. Social codes were implicitly followed. Less than 10% of the loans were in default.

Why do the villagers trust one another? They do, because agreements are mutually enforced: a threat by members of a community that stiff sanctions will be imposed on anyone breaking an agreement would deter everyone from breaking it. This is a common basis for doing business in the poor world. Among the Kofyar farmers in Nigeria, for example, agricultural land is privatized, but free-range grazing is permitted once the crops have been harvested. Like Desta's household, Kofyar households are engaged in subsistence farming, so labor isn't paid a wage. However, unlike Desta's village, where household farms manage on their own labor, the Kofyars have instituted communal work on individual farms. Although some of this is organized in clubs of eight to ten individuals, there are also community-wide work parties. A household that doesn't provide the required quota of labor without good excuse is fined (as it happens, in jars of beer). If fines aren't paid, errant households are punished by being denied communal labor and subjected to social ostracism. In a different context, systems of codes have served to protect fisheries in coastal villages of northern Brazil. Violations are met with a range of sanctions that include both shunning and sabotaging fishing equipment. And so on.

How is mutual enforcement able to support agreements? It is all well and good to say that sanctions will be imposed on opportunists, but why should the threats be believed? They would be believed if sanctions were an aspect of social norms of behavior. To see why, assume for the moment that whether an agreement has been kept by each party is *observable* by all parties.

No doubt this is a strong assumption, but as with "verifiability," it is a useful starting point. Once we draw conclusions from it, we will be able to infer how communities could modify their institutions in situations where the assumption doesn't hold even approximately. That said, anyone who has visited villages in poor countries will know that privacy is not a fundamental right there. In tropical villages that I have visited, cottages are designed and clustered in such a fashion that it must be hard for anyone to prevent others from observing what they are about.

By a social norm we mean an accepted rule of behavior. A rule of behavior reads like: "I will do X if you do Y"; "I will do P if Q happens"; and so forth. For a rule of behavior to *be* a social norm, it must be in the interest of each person to act in accordance with the rule if all others act in accordance with it; that is, the rule should correspond to a Nash equilibrium. To see how social norms work, let us return to our numerical example to study whether cooperation based on a *long-term relationship* can be sustained between A (we now call him the patron) and B (we now call her the client).

Imagine that the opportunity for A and B to do business with each other is expected to arise over and over again; say, annually. The time taken for B to produce her output is assumed to be well within a year. Let t denote time. So t assumes the values 0, 1, 2, . . . , and so on, *ad infinitum*; with 0 standing for the current year, 1 standing for the following year, 2 standing for the year following that, and so on, *ad infinitum*. Although the future benefits from cooperation are important to both A and B, they will typically be less important than present benefits. After all, there is always the chance that one of the parties will not be around in the future to continue the relationship, or that circumstances may change in such ways that A does not have access to his capital flow. To formalize this idea, we introduce a positive number r, which measures the rate at which either party discounts the future benefits from cooperation. (We will see that in the present example, it doesn't matter what B's discount rate is. For expositional ease, though, I assume that both individuals discount their future costs and benefits at the rate r.) The assumption is that, when making calculations in the current year (which is $t = 0$), each divides his or her benefits in any future year t by a factor $(1 + r)^t$. (The term $(1 + r)^t$ denotes $(1 + r)$ multiplied to itself t times.) So, if r is positive, $(1 + r)^t$ exceeds unity for all future t; and since benefits in year t are divided by $(1 + r)^t$ when making calculations in the current year, the importance of those benefits decays by a fixed percentage r each year when viewed from today. The smaller is r, the greater is the weight placed on the benefits of future cooperation. We now show that, provided r is small, the pair could in principle enter a successful long-term relationship, where each year A advances \$4,000 to B, sells the goods B has produced for \$8,000, and pays her \$3,000. The formal theory of long-term relationships was developed by the mathematicians Robert Aumann and Lloyd Shapley, and extended by the economists Drew Fudenberg, Eric Maskin, Ariel Rubinstein, and others. What I present here is an illustration of how the theory works.

Consider the following rule of behavior that A might adopt: (i) begin by advancing \$4,000 to B, (ii) sell the goods if she produces them during the year, (iii) share the proceeds according to the agreement, and (iv) continue doing so every year so long as neither party has broken the agreement; but (v) end the relationship permanently the year following the first defection by either party. Similarly, consider the following rule of behavior that B might adopt: so long as neither party has reneged on the agreement, work faithfully for A each year; but refuse ever to work for him the year following the first violation of the agreement by either party.

The two rules embody a common idea: begin by cooperating and continue to cooperate so long as neither party has broken their word, but withdraw cooperation permanently following the first defection from the agreement by either party. Withdrawal of cooperation is the sanction. Game theorists have christened this most unforgiving of rules the "grim strategy," or simply *grim*. We show next that grim is capable of supporting the long-term relationship if r is not too large.

First consider *B*. She will be willing to enter into the agreement so long as $1,000/r$ exceeds $2,000; that is, so long as r is less than 50% a year. Let us assume it is. Suppose *A* has adopted grim and *B* believes that he has. He will advance her the capital at the beginning of year 0. *B*'s best course of actions is clear: keep to the agreement. For suppose she reneges on the agreement. She would lose $1,000 (her share of $3,000 minus the $2,000 she would earn producing home goods), but gain nothing in any future year (remember, *A* has adopted grim). This means she couldn't do better than to adopt grim if *A* has adopted grim.

The harder piece of reasoning is *A*'s. Suppose *B* has adopted grim and *A* believes she has. If he has advanced the working capital to her, she will have worked faithfully for him in year 0. *A* now wonders what to do. If he reneges on the agreement, he would earn $8,000 (the $4,000 he could have earned with his capital even if he had not entered into the relationship with *B* would be bygones by year 1). But since he believes *B* to have adopted grim, he must also believe that *B* will retaliate by never working for him again. So, set against a single year's gain of $8,000 is a net loss of $[5,000/(1 + r) − 4,000]$, which is the foregone profit from the partnership every year, starting year 1. That loss is the sum, $[(1,000 − 4,000r)/(1 + r) + (1,000 − 4,000r)/(1 + r)^2 + \ldots$ *ad infinitum*$)$, which can be shown to add up to $(1,000 − 4,000r)/r$. If $(1,000 − 4,000r)/r$ exceeds 8,000, it isn't in *A*'s interest to break the agreement, which means that he can't do better than to adopt grim himself. But $(1,000 - 4,000r)/r$ exceeds 8,000 if and only if r is less than $1/12$ per year. We have therefore proved that if r is less than $1/12$ per year, it is in each party's interest to adopt grim if the other party adopts grim. But if both adopt grim, neither would be the first to defect, which implies that the agreement would be kept. We have therefore proved that grim can serve as a social norm to maintain a long-term relationship between the patron (A) and the client (B).

Economists have found evidence of grim in social interchanges, but it would appear to be in force mostly where people also have access to formal markets. In Desta's world, though, grim is not in evidence. Sanctions are graduated, the first misdemeanor being met by a small punishment, subsequent ones by a stiffer punishment, persistent ones by a punishment that is stiffer still, and so forth. How are we to explain this?

Where formal markets and long-term relationships coexist, grim could be expected to be in operation. Grim involves permanent sanctions, which is a needed device for preventing people from engaging in opportunistic behavior when good short-term opportunities appear nearby from time to time. But if, as in Desta's village, there are few alternatives to long-term relationships, communitarian arrangements would be of high value to all. Adopting grim would be an overkill in a world where people discount the future benefits from cooperation at a low rate. For that reason, the norms that are adopted involve less draconian sanctions than grim. A single misdemeanor is interpreted as an error on the part of the defector, or as "testing the water" (to check if others were watching). This is why graduated sanctions are frequently observed.

Here then is our general finding: social norms of behavior are able to sustain cooperation if people care sufficiently about the future benefits of cooperation. The precise terms and conditions will be expected to vary across time and place; what is common to them all is that cooperation is mutually enforced, it isn't based on external enforcement.

There is, however, a piece of bad news: people could end up not cooperating even if they care a lot about the future benefits of cooperation. To see how, imagine that each party believes that all others will renege on the agreement. It would then be in each one's interest to renege at once, meaning that there would be no cooperation. Even if r is less than 1/12 per year in our numerical example, behavior amounting to non-cooperation is also a Nash equilibrium: A doesn't advance the $4,000 worth of raw material to B, because he knows that B won't work for him; she would refuse because of the fear that A won't keep his promise to share the proceeds, a fear that is justified, given that A intends not to share the $8,000 with her once she has produced those goods; and so on. Failure to cooperate could be due simply to an unfortunate pair of self-confirming beliefs, nothing else. No doubt it is mutual suspicion that ruins their chance to cooperate, but the suspicions are internally self-consistent. In short, even when appropriate institutions are in place to enable people to cooperate, they may not do so. Whether they cooperate depends on mutual beliefs, nothing more. I have known this result for many years, but still find it a surprising and disturbing fact about social life.

Could the pair form a partnership if r exceeds 1/12 per year? The answer is "no." As grim is totally unforgiving, no other rule could inflict a heavier sanction for a single misdemeanor. The temptation A faces to defect is less if B adopts grim than if she were to adopt any other rule of behavior; which implies that no rule of behavior could support a partnership if r exceeds 1/12 per year. Studying grim is useful, because it allows us in many examples, such as the present one, to determine the largest value of r for which cooperation is possible.

We now have in hand a tool to explain how a community can skid from cooperation to non-cooperation. Ecological stress—caused, for example, by increasing population and prolonged droughts—often results in people fighting over land and natural resources (Chapter 7). Political instability—in the extreme, civil war—could in turn be a reason why both A and B become concerned that A's source of capital will be destroyed or confiscated. A would now discount the future benefits of cooperation with B at a higher rate. Similarly, if the two fear that their government is now more than ever bent on destroying communitarian institutions in order to strengthen its own authority, r would rise. For whatever reason, if r were to rise beyond 1/12 per year, the relationship would break down. Mathematicians call the points at which those switches occur *bifurcations*. Sociologists call them *tipping points*. Social norms work only when people have reasons to value the future benefits of cooperation.

Contemporary examples illustrate this. Local institutions have been observed to deteriorate in the unsettled regions of sub-Saharan Africa. Communal management systems that once protected Sahelian forests from unsustainable use were destroyed by governments keen to establish their authority over rural people. But Sahelian officials had no expertise at forestry, nor did they have the resources to observe who took what from the forests. Many were corrupt. Rural communities were unable to switch from communal governance to governance based on the law: the former was destroyed and the latter didn't really get going. The collective vacuum has had a terrible impact on people whose lives had been built round their forests and woodlands.

Ominously, there are subtler pathways by which societies can tip from a state of mutual trust to one of mutual distrust. Our model of the partnership between A and B has shown that when r is less than 1/12 per year, both cooperation and non-cooperation are equilibrium outcomes. The example therefore tells us that a society could tip over from cooperation to non-cooperation owing merely to a change in beliefs. The tipping may have nothing to do with any discernible change in circumstances; the entire shift in behavior could be triggered in people's minds. The switch could occur quickly and unexpectedly, which is why it would be impossible to predict and why it would cause surprise and dismay. People who woke up in the morning as friends would discover at noon that they are at war with one another. Of course, in practice there are usually cues to be found. False rumors and propaganda create pathways by which people's beliefs can so alter that they tip a society where people trust one another to one where they don't.

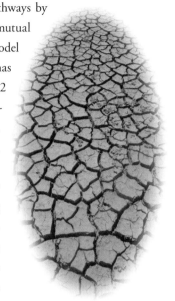

A dry lakebed in Chad, where the Sahel region meets the expanding Sahara Desert, indicates how precious resources are vanishing as a result of deforestation and unsustainable farming practices.

The reverse can happen too, but it takes a lot longer. Rebuilding a community that was previously racked by civil strife involves building trust. Non-cooperation doesn't require as much coordination as cooperation does. Not to cooperate usually means to withdraw. To cooperate, people must not only trust one another to do so, they also have to coordinate on a social norm that everyone understands. That is why it's a lot easier to destroy a society than to build it.

How does an increase or decrease in cooperation translate into macroeconomic statistics? Our numerical example captured a salient point, that an increase in cooperation raises incomes by permitting a more efficient allocation of resources: A's working capital was put to better use under cooperation, as was B's labor. Consider now two communities that are identical in all respects, excepting that in one people have coordinated

A US Army soldier burns a Viet Cong base camp during the Vietnam War (1959–75). While a brief period of conflict can leave society in ruins—as in Vietnam, where millions died—a much greater time is needed to rebuild.

at an equilibrium where they trust one another, while people in the other have coordinated at an equilibrium where they don't trust one another. The difference between the two economies would be reflected in their total factor productivity, which would be higher in the community where people trust one another than in the one where they don't. Enjoying greater income, individuals in the former economy are able to put aside more of their income to accumulate capital assets, other things being equal. So GDP growth there is higher. Mutual trust would be interpreted from the statistics as a driver of economic growth.

Communities and Markets

How did people who now interact with one another get to connect in the first place? In Desta's village the answer is simple: mostly they have known one another from birth. People engaged in long-term relationships based on social norms—*communities*, for short—have to know one another, at least indirectly, through people they know personally. Desta's father, for example, knows most members of the *iddir* to which he belongs. The family knows all those with whom they share the local commons. Communities are *personal* and *exclusive*. Members have names, personalities, and attributes. An outsider's word isn't as good as an insider's.

In contrast, the hallmark of transactions enforced by the law of contracts is that they can take place among people who don't know one another. In Becky's world, people are mobile, a pattern of behavior not unrelated to the fact that they are able to do business even with people they don't know. Becky frequently doesn't know the salespersons in the department stores of her town's shopping mall, nor do they know Becky. When Becky's parents borrow from their bank, the funds made available to them come from unknown depositors. Literally millions of transactions take place each day among people who have never met and will never meet. Often, the exchanges take place only once, unlike exchanges based on long-term relationships. *Markets* are prime examples of institutions offering such opportunities. In contrast to communities, markets are *impersonal* and *inclusive*. Witness the oft-used phrase: "My money is as good as yours."

Property Rights

Property rights to a commodity are the rights, restrictions, and privileges regarding its use. The subject is central to economics because it is closely related to the incentives people have to use goods and services in one way rather than another. Ill-defined property rights to a commodity usually spell bad news, because no one is fully able to capture the benefits that can be obtained from it; which is another way of saying that, all things considered, no one has an incentive to put the commodity to its most efficient use. For brevity, we will assume that ownership of a commodity includes (i) the right to use it in the way the owner chooses and (ii) the right to exchange it for some other commodity (by selling or leasing it) or to offer it as a gift.

In talking of property rights, we shouldn't only mean *private* property. There are a number of commodities in Desta's village that are *communally* owned. Desta's community has historical rights to them. They are called "common property resources" (*CPRs*), or simply the "local commons." CPRs are frequently natural resources (grazing fields, ponds, woodlands, coastal fisheries, mangrove swamps). But produced goods can be CPRs, too. For example, villagers in the microwatersheds of poor countries have been known to build catchments that serve both as irrigation tanks and as fisheries. The tanks were built and are maintained by collective effort. They are regarded by villagers as CPRs. Where they are communally managed, CPRs aren't open to all, but only to those having historical rights. As the transactions involving them are typically not mediated by market prices, their fate can go unreported in national economic accounts (Chapter 7).

There is, however, a bad piece of news about institutions that regulate the use of CPRs. Entitlements to products from CPRs are frequently based on private land holdings: richer households enjoy a greater proportion of the benefits from the local commons. Access to the more productive bits of CPRs in India are not infrequently restricted to caste Hindus. That women are sometimes excluded has also been recorded—for example, from communal forestry. Communities can be as ruthless as markets.

CPRs are to be distinguished from goods to which there is *open access*. The latter category consists of commodities that belong to everyone, meaning that they belong to no one. Except for the case of knowledge about "facts of nature" (Chapter 5), it is unusual for someone to produce something and then allow free access to it; which is why commodities to which there is open access are typically unconfined natural resources, such as the atmosphere and the open seas.

A Kenyan girl carries home firewood, often collected from local commons, property that is communally owned and to which the villagers have an historical right of use.

Even when ownership isn't in dispute, it can be that a property is managed badly. This can happen if, for example, those who own it are unable to cooperate (an unmanaged CPR), or if those who manage the property resort to corrupt practices (inflating a firm's profits by dubious accounting practices), or if directors of companies make decisions that are not in the interest of shareholders. So long as community members don't discount the future benefits of cooperation at too high a rate, collective agreements over the use of CPRs can be made credible by recourse to social norms of behavior. Why then do people typically fail to reach agreement on the use of open access resources? The answer is that cooperation would involve too many people with differing needs and intentions. Moreover, as cheaper ways for extracting natural resources are discovered and economic growth is accompanied by ever increasing waste material that must find room somewhere, the extraction rate under open access increases. These factors explain why fisheries in the open seas and the atmosphere as a sink for carbon emissions are under severe stress today. Open access resources are overused, because no one has to pay for the right to use them.

The Bear Stearns office tower in New York City was a symbol of the investment bank's affluence and financial power until the company foundered in 2008 as a result of the subprime mortgage crisis. Bear Stearns was bought by J. P. Morgan that year, escaping bankruptcy.

Whether ownership is private, communal, or whether it is "open access" depends in part on the commodity's characteristics. Mobile resources are difficult to privatize, but some can be prevented from becoming open to free access. Communities have been known to share river water, and coastal fisheries are often CPRs. Agreements are kept either by an external enforcer or by mutual enforcement. The context matters.

It is no accident that as much as 20% of Desta's household income is from the local commons, whereas the CPR in Becky's neighborhood provides households there with the opportunity at best to picnic. Historical studies tell us that CPRs decline in importance as economies grow. They decline because the relative scarcities of goods and services change with economic growth. Compared to manufactured capital and human capital, land is pretty much fixed in size. Moreover, scientific and technological advances make available more and more productive uses for land. Some people want to develop the land for one set of purposes, others for other purposes. As it becomes ever harder for communities to reach agreement over the use of land-based CPRs, the urge to privatize grows.

Goods and Services: Classifications

It is good practice to distinguish one object from another if they happen to be distinct. Goods and services are commonly distinguished from one another by their physical and chemical properties (for example, potable water is different from wheat). People generally acknowledge that goods and services should be distinguished from one another also by their location, as is implicit in the disparagement that someone is "bringing coals to Newcastle." Thus, potable water in the Sahara is a different commodity from potable water in Alaska. The economist Erik Lindahl showed many years ago that to make sense of borrowing, saving, lending, and investing

Sand dunes rise beyond an oasis in the Saharan city of Ubari, Libya. Oases, which provide access to precious potable water, have historically been crucial to desert trade routes between African communities.

(Chapter 6), we should distinguish goods and services from one another also by the date of their appearance. As potable water today is a different commodity from potable water tomorrow, we should acknowledge the difference. It follows from Lindahl's account that a durable commodity should be regarded as the stream of services it is expected to provide over time.

The economist Kenneth Arrow showed that commodities should be distinguished from one another even more finely. He argued that in order to make sense of insurance and the stock market, we should distinguish goods and services from one another also by the uncertain contingencies in which they appear. It follows from Arrow's account that potable water tomorrow in case the weather will be cold is a different commodity from potable water tomorrow in case it will be hot.

Planning for the future requires that we make provisions of goods and services at future dates. When a trader in Becky's world buys wheat forward—that is, he pays now for a bushel, to be delivered in six weeks' time, say—he buys wheat of a certain composition (kernel size, moisture content, and so forth), to be delivered in six weeks' time, no matter what. By storing maize in their home, Desta's parents try to ensure that the

Stanford economist Kenneth
Arrow is one of the defining
architects of modern economic
analysis. Arrow's pioneering
contributions to the field include
study of the processes by which
resources are allocated in
decentralized economies. His
work in "social choice theory"
has transformed understanding
of the underlying logic of
democratic voting procedures.

household is able to consume maize until near the next harvest, no matter what. In terms of Lindahl's classification, both the trader and Desta's parents are purchasing "dated commodities." But the future is inevitably uncertain. By paying an annual insurance premium on their home, Becky's parents purchase a replacement for their home during the following year *if and only if* their home is damaged. (They don't get the premium refunded should their home remain undamaged at the end of the year.) The commodity they are buying is a home that replaces the present one during the following year if and only if their present home is damaged. In Arrow's terminology, they are purchasing a "contingent commodity."

Private Goods, Public Goods, and Externalities

By a *private good* economists mean a commodity whose use is both rivalrous and excludable. Food is a quintessential private good. If someone consumes an additional unit of food from a given amount, all others taken together will have a unit less to consume (that's "rivalrous"); and so long as the rights to the food someone possesses are protected, he or she can exclude others from consuming any of it (that's "excludable"). Most of the goods we consume or use are, in this sense, private. In sharp contrast, a *public good* is a commodity whose use is *non*-rivalrous and *non*-excludable. National defense comes readily to mind. If a nation has the equipment to protect itself against attack, it not only protects all who live there, it would cost nothing more to protect anyone else who comes to live there (that's "non-rivalrous"); moreover, it wouldn't be possible to exclude anyone who comes to live there from that protection (that's "non-excludable"). There are public "bads" as well. Effluence from paper mills is a ready example.

Public goods are the mirror image of resources to which access is open. In contrast to open access resources, which are overused, public goods are undersupplied if people are left to their own devices. The economists Knut Wicksell and Paul Samuelson traced the reason for that undersupply to the incentives people have to *free-ride* on the provisions others happen to make. The point is that once a public good is supplied, it is a commodity to which access is open. But the private incentive to supply the good won't take that benefit into account. Wicksell and Samuelson argued that the problem can be overcome only by collective action. That action can take one of two forms: (i) public provision; (ii) publicly subsidized private provision. Where the geographical reach of a public good is confined (forest cover in microwatersheds; local sewage systems), "public" may mean the community or the local government. In either case we are in the realm of local politics. In Desta's world, local public goods are usually supplied by the community; in Becky's, they are the responsibility of local government. In neither world does the market take the lead. Where the public good is confined within a national boundary (national defense), collective action means state involvement, and so, national politics. When the public good is unconfined (the global circulation system governing climate), collective action can only mean involvement of the international community, and so, international politics.

The private provision of public goods confers an extreme form of an effect known as *externalities*. By an externality, we mean the effects that decisions have on people who have not been party to the decisions. In some cases the effects are beneficial (they are known as *positive* externalities); in other cases they are detrimental (*negative* externalities). Primary education and public health measures confer positive externalities. If I become literate, I benefit; but so do others who are literate, because they can now communicate with me via non-oral means. Similarly, if I get inoculated against an infectious disease, I benefit; but so do others who are susceptible to the disease, because they are no longer in danger from me. Imagine now that education and inoculation are institutionalized as private goods. Each household would underinvest in both, because none would take into account the benefits they would be conferring on others.

In contrast, crowding on highways and particulates in a city's air shed involve negative externalities. If you drive your car on the highway, presumably you benefit; but you add to congestion and so cause others to suffer on the highway. Similarly, when your car emits particulates, others living under the air shed suffer a loss. Each such case involves the free-rider problem, much referred to by political commentators today. The idea that free-riding and externalities are related is old. The economist A. C. Pigou noted the problem in the 1920s and advocated the use of taxes and subsidies, respectively, for reducing the private supply of negative externalities and increasing the private supply of positive externalities.

Money

By subsistence agriculture, economists mean self-sufficient agrarian households. Desta's household isn't quite like that, but it is close enough. Becky's household is very different. Her parents' income is used to obtain the goods and services her household consumes. The household does that by trading in the market. If you were to itemize the number of transactions Becky's household makes each year, the vast majority—consisting mostly of very small items, such as groceries—are for immediate consumption. Payments in Becky's world are made in money, expressed in US dollars. The notes and coins that form a part of what goes by the name "money" possess no intrinsic worth. So why do people hold them? Why do we need a medium of exchange in the first place?

Imagine a world where everyone is known to be utterly trustworthy; where people don't incur any cost in computing, remembering, and recognizing people; and where every transaction—whether here and now, or across time, space, and uncertain contingencies—can be carried out costlessly. In that world people would be able to do business with one another merely on the basis of their word. There would be no need for money.

We don't live in that world. To see why money is a necessary medium of exchange in the world we live in, imagine that person A possesses wheat, person B rice, and person C maize. Let us suppose also that A likes rice, B maize, and C wheat. Bilateral exchanges of goods (more commonly known as "barter") would be impossible because of an absence of what economists call a "double-coincidence of wants": *A* wants *B*'s rice but can't barter with *B* because *B* doesn't care for *A*'s wheat; and so on. The example is stark, but the problem it poses is very general. The use of money as a medium of exchange enables people to do business with one another even in the absence of a double-coincidence of wants. Money is a legal tender in both Becky's and Desta's worlds because the governments in their countries say it is a legal tender and back that statement with the power of their authority. Paul Samuelson constructed a model not dissimilar to the one we studied earlier (of a partnership between persons *A* and *B*) to show that, although money is intrinsically value-less, people hold money because they want to be able to purchase goods and services without possessing goods and services with which to barter. So money is not only a medium of exchange, but also a store of value. Becky's household wouldn't be able to survive if it didn't live in a monetary economy. Desta's household, being nearly self-sufficient, could just about survive. However, we should avoid imputing causality when there is none. If Becky's household lived in a place where markets were absent, it too would try to be self-sufficient. The family would be destitute if her father tried to live on his skills as a lawyer. Of course, even Desta's parents need money to purchase the goods available in the few markets that exist in their village environment. They accept money in exchange for the liquor Desta's mother brews and the *teff* her father grows.

Notes and coins issued by the government are not the only kind of money in Becky's world. Business transactions most often use checks drawn from one bank to another. As current account balances also serve as a medium of exchange, they are also money. When signing a contract, the relevant parties entertain certain beliefs about the dollar's future value, by which I mean beliefs concerning the bundles of goods and services a dollar will purchase in the future. Those beliefs are based in part on their trust—more accurately, *confidence*—in the US government to manage the value of the dollar. Of course, the beliefs are based on many other things besides, but the important point remains that money's value is maintained only because people believe it will be maintained. Similarly if, for whatever reason, people fear that the value will not be maintained, then it won't be maintained. Currency crashes, such as the one that occurred in Weimar Germany in 1922–3, are an illustration of how a loss in confidence can be self-confirming. Bank runs share that feature, as do stock market bubbles and crashes. There are multiple social equilibria, each supported by a set of self-confirming beliefs. One of the most important purposes of monetary policy is to maintain the value of money.

Money enables transactions to be anonymous. Those anonymous transactions are concluded in one go, as when Becky buys CDs in the department store of her town's shopping mall and pays for the purchases

A banknote for five hundred thousand marks was worth less than one US dollar in 1923, after the collapse of Weimar Germany's economy.

in cash. Millions of transactions take place each day between people who have never met and will never meet. The problem of trust is in great part solved in Becky's world by building confidence in the medium of exchange: money.

Because of an absence of good roads, electricity, and running water, markets are unable to penetrate Desta's village. Becky's suburban town, in contrast, is embedded in a gigantic world economy. Becky's father is able to specialize as a lawyer only because he is assured that his income can be used to purchase food in the supermarket, water from the tap, and heat from cooking ovens and radiators. Specialization enables people to produce more in total than they would be able to if they were each required to diversify their activities. Adam Smith famously remarked that the division of labor is limited by the extent of the market. Earlier we noted that Desta's household doesn't specialize, but produces pretty much all daily requirements from a raw state. Moreover, the many transactions it enters into with others, being supported by social norms, are of necessity personalized, thus limited. There is a world of a difference between markets and communities as the basis of economic activities because there is a world of a difference between laws and social norms.

Culture

The models we have been studying capture those all-too-familiar situations where cooperation requires institutions (arrangements for implementing agreements, which specify who is to keep an eye on whom, who is to report to whom, and so forth), but where non-cooperation is a possible outcome even when those institutions are in place. We know that certain institutions work smoothly in some places, but not in others. A nation may adopt an enlightened constitution, but whether its citizens can bring themselves to work within it is a different matter. What people choose to do depends, among other things, on their beliefs about one another. The theory I am developing here doesn't explain those beliefs; what it does is to identify those that are self-confirming. Economists call them *rational beliefs*. Nothing philosophically deep is meant by the term *rational* here: rational beliefs are beliefs that are self-confirming, nothing more. The models have also told us that, in a wide variety of everyday situations, rational beliefs are not unique. Some give rise to outcomes that protect and promote human well-being, others thwart it. What gives rise to one set of rational beliefs rather than another? Could it be culture?

German sociologist Max Weber's
Die protestantische Ethik und der Geist des Kapitalismus (The Protestant Ethic and the Spirit of Capitalism)—Weber's most influential work in the field of economics—advanced the argument that religious ethics played a key role in the development of capitalism.

In his famous work on the influence of culture on economic development, the sociologist Max Weber took a community's culture to be its shared values and dispositions, not just beliefs. Studies as widely cast as Weber's can't easily be summarized, but the causal mechanism Weber himself would seem to have favored in his work on the Protestant ethic and the spirit of capitalism leads from religion, through personal practices and political culture, to institutions, and thereby to economic outcomes.

Using culture to explain economic performance hasn't been popular among social scientists in recent decades; but there has been a revival. For example, economists have constructed a measure of trust in societies from the World Values Survey, which in the early 1980s and 1990s surveyed 1,000 randomly selected individuals in each of 40 countries and asked them if, generally speaking, they would say that most people could be trusted or that they could not be too careful in dealing with people. Trust was measured by the percentage who replied that most people could be trusted (the percentages were found to be pretty much the same in the two surveys). The investigators controlled for differences in GDP per head among the countries that were surveyed. The data revealed that trust, on the one hand, and judicial efficiency, tax compliance, bureaucratic quality, civic participation, infant survival rate, educational achievement, the performance of large firms, and growth in GDP per head, on the other hand, moved together. In statistical jargon, they were positively (and significantly) correlated. Not surprisingly, the data also revealed that trust and government corruption moved together, but in opposite directions. The two variables were negatively (and significantly) correlated.

We could conclude from the World Values Survey that trust is good for economic growth and several other good things besides. But the survey didn't identify the reasons why the degree of trust in each of the countries sampled was what it was. Nor *could* it identify the reasons. This poses a problem. As trust doesn't get created in a vacuum, its presence cries out for explanation. Which means that the presence of trust shouldn't be used to explain the presence of something else. What the statistical findings tell us is that such emergent features of an economy as the degree of trust people have in one another go hand in hand with economic progress, they tell us nothing more. Statisticians remind the rest of us repeatedly that correlation isn't the same as causation. It is an instruction social commentators have all too often ignored.

That said, to have observed a positive correlation between trust and economic progress is informative because the theory we have been developing here predicts positive correlation. If the correlation had been *negative*, we would have been utterly surprised. We would have questioned the finding and gone back to the drawing board, either by redoing the survey, or by trying to identify hidden variables in the data that could account for it.

All this is in line with a train of thought regarding institutions that I have been exploring here, that long-term relationships are often *substitutes* for trust in government officials to deliver public services or for confidence in the ability of formal markets to function adequately. Perhaps people enter into long-term relationships when the other institutions that could serve similar purposes are unreliable.

In addition to questions on trust, the World Values Survey contained a list of character traits and practices, including thrift, saving money and objects, determination, obedience, and religious faith. The survey asked people to identify the one they regarded as the most important. Based on their responses, political scientists have constructed an index of culture that reflects the personal motivation to achieve. Controlling for other factors, differences in economic growth and the index of personal motivation were found to go together—they were positively and significantly correlated.

This finding shouldn't be given a causal interpretation either. The motivation to advance oneself could depend on one's expectations regarding the chance that hard work pays off. Parents would instill personal ambition in their children only if they were sanguine that such ambition would not be thwarted by the social order. Women wouldn't rise beyond their station if they (rationally!) feared retaliation against them for their temerity. Even an attitude can be a determined rather than determining factor. When it's the former, an observed statistical link between the culture of, say, thrift and economic progress should be interpreted as a relationship, nothing more. I am using the term *culture* here to denote differences in the beliefs people hold about one another. Culture in this view is a coordinating device.

Attitudes toward others and toward one's institutions are significant aspects of a society's culture. The models we have studied so far have focused on the latter. In what follows we look at the former, by studying socially influential behavior.

Socially Influential Behavior

The fertility rate (TFR) in Desta's world is more than twice as high as in Becky's world (Table 1). What accounts for the huge difference?

In Chapter 6 we will explore such factors as the costs and benefits parents experience from having children and the relative ease with which households have access to modern reproductive technology and health care. Here we focus on socially influential behavior as a possible factor. Conformity is one example. By conformity, I mean imitative, or herd, behavior. Reproductive behavior is *conformist* if, other things being equal, each household's most desired size is larger, the greater is the average household size in the group with which it identifies.

In Figure 1 on page 76, I have drawn a hypothetical curve, *AB*, which reflects the dependence of the average household's desired fertility rate (Y) on the community's fertility rate (X). It is upward-sloping, reflecting conformist behavior. I have so drawn *AB* that it intersects the 45-degree line at three values of X: 2, 4, 7. The hypothetical community would be at a reproductive equilibrium at each intersection: as long as the community's fertility rate is 7, the average household would most desire 7; but if it is 2, the average household would desire 2. So, conformism can be the reason for the existence of multiple reproductive equilibria. This means that communities that are separated from each other, but are otherwise identical, could behave very differently. In our example, it could be that the TFR in some communities is 2, while in others it is 7. (A TFR of 4 is also a reproductive equilibrium, but it is unstable, meaning that if a community's TFR were ever so slightly different from 4, it would diverge from 4 even more with time.)

People tend to identify with more than one group. Often, our food habits have been acquired from our parents, our work habits influenced by those in our profession, our leisure habits by our class,

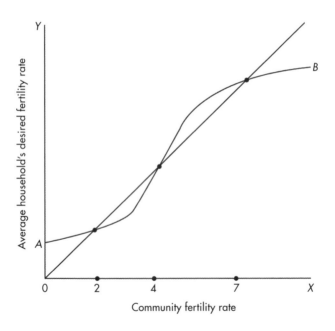

Figure 1. This graph shows the relationship between the average household's desired fertility rate and the community's fertility rate.

and our reproductive goals by our religion or ethnic background. It may be that we conform because we care about our status, and our actions signal our willingness to be a part of our group. No matter what the basis of conformism happens to be, there would be practices encouraging high fertility rates that no household would unilaterally wish to break. Those practices could have had a rationale in the past, when mortality rates were high, rural population densities were low, the threat of extermination from outside attack was large, and mobility was restricted. But practices can survive even when their original purposes have disappeared, especially perhaps if people look over their shoulders at what others are doing before deciding what they themselves will do.

Conformist behavior would change over time if the reference group on whose behavior households base their own decisions changes. Even within a group there are those who experiment, take risks, and refrain from joining the crowd. They are the tradition-breakers, often leading the way. Demographers have noted that educated women are among the first to make the move toward smaller families. Middle-class behavior can also be the trigger for change. A possibly even stronger pathway is the influence newspapers, radio, television, and the Internet exert by transmitting information about lifestyles elsewhere. In other words, the media can be a vehicle by which conformism increasingly becomes based on the behavior of a wider population than the local community: the reference group widens. Increased conformity with the behavior of people in distant lands can even be mistaken for growth in individualism. We now have the beginnings of a theory of *demographic transitions*, by which we mean a relatively brief period of time during which the TFR cascades down from a high figure to a relatively low figure. In recent years there have been signs of demographic transitions even in parts of sub-Saharan Africa, where the TFR has dropped from 7–8 to 4–5. But there remain parts of the continent where the TFR remains nearly 8.

In her study of demographic change in Western Europe over the period 1870–1960, Susan Cotts Watkins found that in 1870, before the large-scale declines in marital fertility had begun in most areas of Western Europe, demographic behavior differed greatly within countries. The fertility rate among provinces (counties, cantons) differed considerably, even while differences within provinces were low. There were spatial clusters within each country, suggesting the importance of the influence of local communities on behavior. By 1960, though, differences within each country were less than they had been in 1870. Watkins explained this convergence in behavior in terms of increases in the geographical reach national governments enjoyed over the ninety years in question. The growth of national languages could have been the medium through which reproductive behavior spread.

More transient forms of herd behavior are fads and fashions. Imagine that each person can choose one of two actions, P and Q. Suppose that everyone has an intrinsic preference for P, but that people also like to conform. To model this, imagine that each person would choose P over Q if the proportion of people choosing Q is expected to be less than 65%, but that each person would choose Q over P if the proportion is expected to exceed 65%. The figure 65% is a *critical mass*. (Mathematicians would call the critical mass a *separatrix*.) Once again, simple herd behavior could lead everyone to adopt Q, even though they would all have preferred that everyone had adopted P. A dynamic similar to the one I have just sketched to describe demographic transitions shows that fads and fashions can disappear without much prior notice.

Competitiveness (trying to "keep up with the Joneses") can also lead to socially influential behavior. Surveys in which people in Desta's world were asked to report how happy they were as compared to the past have confirmed that income matters to the very poor: reported happiness was found on average to have increased with rising incomes. But similar surveys have found that income doesn't contribute to happiness among people who have a good deal more than the basic necessities of life. Those who are poorer in Becky's world are certainly less happy; but even though there was economic growth in the periods covered by the samples, the distribution of declared happiness remained pretty much the same.

A possible explanation is that, when income levels are reasonably high, the extent to which someone feels happy is influenced by his income *relative* to the average income of his reference group. In the presence of such a competitive urge, a "rat race" ensues and resources are wasted. The multiple equilibria are of growth rates in incomes. In each equilibrium people grow richer on average and consume more, but don't feel any happier.

THREE

Communities

●

PEOPLE THROUGHOUT HISTORY HAVE been known to devise ingenious ways to cooperate. One way is to make the benefits and burdens in one engagement depend not only on what takes place there, but also on what happens in some other engagement. In Desta's village the same set of households share the local commons, offer one another loans, join the *iddir*, and help one another out in times of need. The interesting point isn't that the same group of people are in a number of long-term relationships (who else is there to form long-term relationships with?), but that the relationships are tied to one another.

A Koli woman carries fish to market in Mumbai, India, where members of the Koli community have traditionally made a living as deep-sea fishermen. The Koli have taken to the courts to win protection from urban development of their seaside fishing villages. Government cooperation with traditional communities can be beneficial for the society as a whole.

Tied Engagements

To see how ties can help, suppose that in the patron–client relationship we studied in the previous chapter, the discount rate A (the patron) uses to value the future benefits of cooperation with B (the client) exceeds 1/12 per year. We know that for want of trust, the pair would be unable to form a partnership. But now imagine that, in addition to the annual flow of \$4,000 worth of working capital A has access to, he has access to an annual flow of a different type of working capital, worth \$3,000 to him. B doesn't have the skills to work with that capital, but someone named C does. The time C would need to work A's capital into a marketable product is worth \$1,000 to her. Like B, person C doesn't have access to the market for products. The product can fetch \$6,000 in the market and A is in a position to procure it. A considers approaching C with a proposal to form a partnership: the \$6,000 would be used first to compensate the pair; the surplus would then be divided equally between them. Each would enjoy a profit of \$1,000 annually. For what values of r is a partnership between them viable?

C would be willing to enter into the arrangement if r is less than 100% a year (that is, if \$1,000/r exceeds \$1,000). We have already assumed it is. We now need to work through A's reasoning. So let us start in year 0. Suppose C has adopted grim. If A advances his capital to her but reneges on the agreement once she has produced the output, he gains \$6,000, because the \$3,000 advance will be bygones by then. Set against it is the \$(4,000/(1 + r) − 3,000) he would lose every year, starting now. That loss is \$(1,000 − 3,000r)/r. If (1,000 − 3,000r)/r is less than 6,000, A will renege. If, on the other hand, (1,000 − 3,000r)/r exceeds 6,000, A can do no better than to adopt grim himself. Since (1,000 − 3,000r)/r exceeds 6,000 if and only if r

is less than 1/9, the pair are able to form a long-term relationship if A's discount rate is less than 1/9 per year. So suppose r *is* less than 1/9. Then A is able to form a relationship with C, but not with B (r exceeds 1/12, remember; and 1/9 exceeds 1/12).

We are now able to show that A could form a relationship with B if the three were to tie the pair of undertakings. Let the proposal be to create both partnerships, but with the understanding that if any party in any year was to act opportunistically, *both* relationships would be terminated. In order to formalize this, let the rule of behavior adopted by B (respectively, C) now read: begin by cooperating with A and C (respectively, B) and continue to cooperate so long as *no one* has broken their agreement, but cease cooperating with everyone following the first defection by any one in either relationship. Similarly, let the rule of behavior adopted by A now read: begin by cooperating with B and C and continue to cooperate so long as *no one* has broken their agreement, but cease cooperating with everyone following the first defection by any one in either relationship. Each of the parties has adopted grim once again, but grim here comes with an added sting.

It's easy enough to confirm that if r is less than 50% a year, B would adopt grim if A and C adopt grim and that C would adopt grim if A and B adopt grim. The interesting exercise is to determine A's incentives to cooperate if B and C adopt grim. As both clients would terminate their relationship with him if he behaved opportunistically with either, A would defect from both relationships if he defects at all. What remains is to calculate A's gains and losses if he defects from both relationships in year 0. If he does, he gains \$14,000 now (\$8,000 from his partnership with B; \$6,000 from his partnership with C). Set against that is the value of all the future benefits from cooperation he will have to forego.

That loss is $(2,000 – 7,000r)/r$. It follows that A can't do better than to adopt grim himself if $14,000 is less than $(2,000 – 7,000r)/r$; which is to say, if r is less than 2/21 a year. Since 2/21 exceeds 1/12 (it lies between 1/12 and 1/9), the condition under which A and B are able to cooperate is weaker. Suppose r is less than 2/21, but greater than 1/12. By tying the relationships, both can be created; whereas, if they are kept separate, only the one between A and C can form. The intuition behind the finding is clear. A faces greater temptation to defect from his agreement with B than the one with C, which is why the circumstances under which a relationship could form with B are more restricted than they are with C (1/12 is less than 1/9). By tying the two relationships, A's temptation to break his relationship with B is reduced (2/21 exceeds 1/12).

While C doesn't lose from the move to tie the partnerships, she doesn't gain either. Only A and B gain. So B has every reason to offer solidarity to C, whom she now regards as a professional comrade. B may even offer a small compensation to C, so as to give her a positive incentive to agree to having the two partnerships tied. In return, C promises to stick by B should A mistreat her. He doesn't do that, of course, but only because he is smart enough to know that C would break up their relationship if he did.

Further refinements are needed when people who wish to trade with one another are separated by distance. Community responsibility systems in Italy during the twelfth and thirteenth centuries helped people to obtain credit and insurance. Transgressions by a party were met in a collective way: the group to which the injured party belonged imposed sanctions on the group of which the transgressor was a member. In such arrangements it is communities, not individuals, that acquire a reputation for honesty. Tying relationships in this manner creates incentives for members of a peer group to keep an eye on one another. The institution reduces the costs people incur in keeping an eye on one another.

The drawback of tied relationships among people having different interests is that they require further coordination. If, in our numerical example, B possessed not only her own skills but those of C as well, and if she had the time to work for A in both ventures, it would be simpler for A to offer both partnerships to B, with the proposal that *they* be tied. The relationship would involve only A and B, requiring less coordination.

Networks

The distinction between personal and impersonal transactions is not sharp. Even in a sophisticated market (modern banking), reputation plays a part (credit rating of the borrower). But the distinction is real. Meeting new people in Becky's world is often accidental, but people spend resources in order to make new acquaintances. Why? One reason is that new acquaintances may be in a position to provide *information*.

One can think of interpersonal networks as systems of communication channels linking people to one another. Networks include as tightly-woven a unit as a nuclear family or kinship group, and one as extensive as a voluntary organization, such as Amnesty International. We are born into certain networks and enter new ones. Personal relationships, whether or not they are long-term, are emergent features within networks.

The clause "personal relationships" in the notion of networks is central. It involves trust without recourse to an external enforcer of agreements. Scholars have argued that civic engagements in Becky's world and communal activities in Desta's world heighten the disposition to cooperate. The idea is that trust begets trust and that this gives rise to a positive feedback between civic and communal activities and a disposition to be so engaged. That positive feedback is, however, tempered by the cost of additional engagements (time), which, typically, rises with increasing engagements. The economist Albert Hirschman has observed that trust is a *moral good*, in that it grows with use but decays with disuse; which means that we don't need to "economize" on trust, in the way we need to with "bread and butter goods" like bread and butter. Trust shares this feature with skills: the more one practices a skill, the better one gets at it.

Weak Ties

Relationships can be strong or weak. One can be misled by this into thinking that weak ties are not valuable. In fact they can be very valuable. While working at his previous job, Becky's father learned through word of mouth that the firm he now works for was looking to hire someone with his qualifications. There is much empirical evidence that weak ties are useful because they connect people to a wide variety of other people, and so, to a large information base. Engagements among people with weak ties in Becky's world are untied. Becky's father has little to do with the Parent-Teacher Association (PTA), of which her mother is an active member. Similarly, Becky's mother has nothing to do with the association of lawyers to which Becky's father belongs. Moreover, neither the PTA nor the Bar Association play any role in their social life.

Strong Ties

In Desta's world ties are mostly strong because they involve tied engagements in long-term relationships. As this sort of arrangement sets limits on the range of people with whom people are able to do business, it offers few opportunities for material advancement. In Chapter 6 we will confirm that strong ties among kinship hinder economic progress in the contemporary world, by limiting the amount of insurance coverage households are able to obtain, by maintaining a low rate of return on investment, and by stimulating fertility. But if used wisely, strong ties can be of help in seeking economic opportunities in the outside world. Consider migration. One enterprising member of the rural community moves to the city, supported by those with whom he has strong ties at home while he searches for work. He is followed by others in a chain-like fashion, as information is sent home of job prospects. Migrant workers even recommend village relations to their bosses. Bosses in turn favor their employees' kin, because doing so reduces the risks involved in hiring people they don't know. This would explain why city mills in poor countries have been found to employ disproportionate numbers of workers from the same village. Markets and communities are capable of functioning in such ways as to offer mutual benefits.

Chinese migrant workers carry their belongings through Beijing. In a pattern encouraged by employers, migrants who find work are soon followed by others from the same rural village.

Why do networks in Desta's world operate along ethnic or kinship lines and why are they multi-purpose and dense, unlike the specialized professional networks such as those of academic economists and psycho-therapists in Becky's world? Our previous analysis offers an answer. As membership is defined by birth, entry into ethnic or kinship networks is impossible, nor is exit possible. Moreover, membership is easily verifiable. Proximity within the village enables individuals to know one another's characteristics and dispositions well. Consequently people there don't suffer much from a problem known in the insurance industry as *adverse selection*. In the insurance context, firms are said to face a problem of "adverse selection" when people who are bad risks are indistinguishable from people who are good risks and are able to displace the latter. Proximity within the village also enables people to observe one another and see what they are about. Consequently people there don't suffer much from a problem known in the insurance industry as *moral hazard*. In the insurance context, firms are said to face a problem of "moral hazard" when insurees don't take those precautions against bad outcomes that may have been agreed upon. Tied long-term relationships make the networks multi-purpose and dense. In contrast, people enter and exit professional networks out of choice, with the result that the networks have sharp, limited goals. Membership doesn't impose constraints on what people can do with other aspects of their lives, such as where to shop, what to eat, which school to send their children.

We shouldn't be surprised that the networks people bequeath their children in Desta's world frequently amount to ethnic or kinship networks, for who else is there in rural societies with whom one can form links? However, even though it is true that exit from one's ethnicity or kinship is literally impossible, children do have a choice of not *using* the networks they have inherited. Why then do people maintain so many inherited networks even in Becky's world? The reason they do is that one can't costlessly redirect relationships once they have been established. Such investments are specific to the relationships. Moreover, as trust begets trust, the cost of maintaining a relationship declines with repeated use (witness that we often take our closest friends and relatives for granted). The benefits from creating new relationships are low if one has inherited a rich network of relationships, which is another way of saying that the cost of not using inherited networks is high. Outside opportunities have to be especially good before it is in someone's interest to cease making use of inherited links. This explains why we maintain so many of the relationships we have inherited from our family and kinship, and why norms of conduct pass down the generations. We are, so to speak, locked in from birth.

Ethiopian farmers winnow *teff,* a nutritious and hardy grain that is a staple in the region.

FOUR

Markets

●

JUST AS COMMUNITIES DIFFER from one another, markets differ from one another. Markets come in so many varieties, that it makes good sense to determine their ideal form and examine why and how actual markets differ from the ideal.

Ideal Markets

Economists refer to departures of markets from their ideal form as "market failure." Each kind of market failure offers society a reason to explore how other institutions, such as households, communities, and government, could improve matters. The argument works the other way, too. Understanding ideal markets enables us to uncover clues as to how markets could improve matters in situations where households, communities, and government don't work so well. Of course, all this presupposes

The ultra-modern Tokyo Stock Exchange hums with activity as commodity traders work the floor.

that ideal markets are a good thing. One of our tasks here is to explore the sense in which they are a good thing.

A Single Market

It helps to begin the formal study of markets by isolating a commodity and developing the account of an ideal market for it. Let us denote the commodity as X. For concreteness, we will suppose that X is a non-durable consumption good, meant for consumption now. As we are studying ideal markets, I assume that X is a private good, implying that there are no externalities associated with its consumption or production. For convenience I will use X also to denote its quantity.

Imagine that there are many firms that could potentially supply X and many households that are potential consumers of X. Firms are owned by households. By a *market* for X we mean a clearing house for X. Firms bring their supplies of X to the market and households arrive there to make their purchases of X. As the markets for goods and services are interconnected (the demand for tea would be expected to increase if the price of coffee was to increase), we would be justified in studying the market for X in isolation only if (i) the resources devoted to the production of X are small compared to the resources devoted to the production of all the other goods and services in the economy, and (ii) the expenditure on X by each household is but a small fraction of its total budget. We make both assumptions here and suppose in addition that all other goods and services are transacted in their own markets. Assumptions (i) and (ii) imply that the prices of all other goods and services are pretty much uninfluenced by what happens in the market for X. That being so, we can value the remaining goods and services in the economy in terms of their prices and sum them so as to create an aggregate index in terms of which

X is priced. Let us call that index *wealth*, expressed in, say, dollars. In the language of economics, wealth is our *numeraire*. Purchases and sales of *X* take place at the price quoted in the market for *X*.

You will no doubt have noticed the circularity in the reasoning I have deployed here. How can we justify assuming in advance of any analysis of the market for *X* that the production and purchases of *X* involve, respectively, only a small proportion of the economy's resources and only a small proportion of each household's budget? By now though, you will have grown used to circular reasoning in economics (Chapter 2). Our previous discussions have shown us that it is a powerful method of analysis. Here we have begun by assuming (i) and (ii). If we now were to discover empirically that near an equilibrium of the market for *X* the assumptions are correct, the basis for the analysis will have been justified.

In an ideal market households and firms are all price-takers. We may imagine that an auctioneer cries out the price of *X* and that firms and households make their respective decisions on the basis of that price. The quantities purchased by each household and sold by each firm are assumed to be verifiable, as is the quality of *X*. Payments are enforced by an external agency (government). People neither steal *X* nor renege on their payments for *X*. If they tried to do either, they would be caught and punished by the enforcer (Chapter 2).

Suppose the price of *X* is *P*. By a household's *demand* for *X* we mean the quantity of the good it would wish to purchase at *P*. If a household's willingness to pay for each unit of *X* declines as the number of units it purchases increases, it would demand the good to the point where its willingness to pay for the marginal unit of *X* equals *P*. (If it demanded more, the household would have to pay more than it was willing to pay for the last unit demanded, meaning that the household would reduce its demand; whereas, if it demanded less, the household would be paying less than it was willing to pay for the last unit demanded, meaning that it would demand still more.) As X is a private good, the *market demand* for X at price P is the sum of all household demands at P. We have just argued that if P were "high," market demand would be "low"; if it were "low," market demand would be "high." This feature gives rise to a downward sloping market demand curve, drawn hypothetically as D' in Figure 2. Market demand for X is measured along the horizontal axis, while P is measured along the vertical axis.

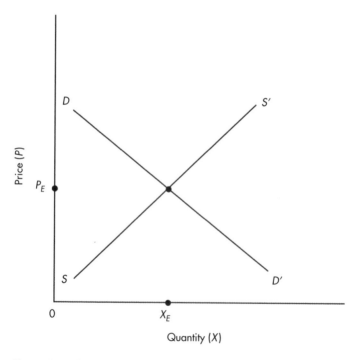

Figure 2. Demand and Supply Curves

It can be that firms own different technologies for producing X. We suppose, though, that all technologies display diminishing returns in production, by which I mean that the cost of producing an additional unit of X (the cost being computed at the prices that prevail for all the inputs required to produce X) increases if the quantity produced was to increase. As firms are owned by households, the objective of every firm is to maximize its profit in the market for X. By a firm's *supply* of X at P we mean the quantity it would be willing to sell at P. A firm would produce the good to the point where the cost it incurs for the last unit produced—its *marginal cost of production*—equals P. (If the firm produced more, it would make a loss on the last unit it produced, which means that it ought to reduce production; whereas, if it produced less, the firm could increase its profit by producing a bit more.) In short, each firm would plan to produce to the point where its marginal cost of production equals P. The *market supply* of X at P is the total quantity of X that all the firms in the economy are willing to supply at P. We have just argued that if P were "high," market supply would be "high"; if it were "low," market supply would be "low." This feature gives rise to the upward sloping market supply curve, drawn hypothetically as S' in Figure 2. Market supply of X is measured along the horizontal axis, while P is measured along the vertical axis.

Figure 2, which was the creation of the economist Alfred Marshall, brings together what is probably the most famous pair of curves in all of economics: the demand and supply curves. The curves intersect at a unique point (X_E units of the good, at price P_E), which is an *equilibrium* of the market for X. It is an equilibrium, because at P_E, market demand equals market supply, implying that the market for X clears. Economists frequently add the adjective "competitive" to the word "equilibrium," because, as the market being studied involves many firms, they are all price-takers. Which is why we say that P_E supports a *competitive equilibrium* in the market for X.

Notice how closely the concept of a competitive equilibrium resembles the notion of an equilibrium in the communities we studied earlier. At P_E, those who wished to be active participants in the market for X—whether as suppliers or purchasers—discover that their intentions can be carried out. Those who chose not to enter the market at that price discover that they were right not to have entered: the market clears at P_E, leaving nothing over which anyone could bargain. P_E enables a set of expectations on the part of households and firms to be fulfilled. Notice too the parsimony of information that households and firms need to have in order to participate effectively in the market for X. A household needs to know its own "mind" (that is, what it is willing to pay for the good) and the price P. It doesn't need to know anything about other households, nor about the cost conditions facing firms. Similarly, a firm needs only to know the technology available to it, the prices it has to pay for its inputs in production, and the price of X. It doesn't need to know anything about households' willingness to pay, nor anything about the technologies of rival firms. The equilibrium price, P_E, acts as a coordinating device for allocating X and the resources needed to produce X. P_E is an emergent feature of the market for X.

In what sense is the market I have just described "ideal"? It is ideal in the sense that the equilibrium supplies and demands would have been chosen by a planner (or regulator), whose objective was to promote household interests by maximizing their joint wealth, and who proceeded to do just that by instructing each firm on how much X to produce and each household on how much X to consume. The proof requires a little bit of patience, but is worth rehearsing. Let us suppose first that the plan the regulator proposes is one in which the marginal costs of production of a pair of firms, 1 and 2, differ; say, the marginal cost for firm 1 exceeds that for firm 2. Total wealth could be increased by a slight change in the regulator's plan: reduce firm 1's output by one unit and raise firm 2's output by one unit. Total output would remain the same, but it would be produced more cheaply, thus increasing the total wealth of households. So, the regulator's best plan—we will call it the *efficient* plan—would involve equality in the marginal cost of production among all those firms that are instructed to produce X.

Turning to households, let us suppose that the plan the regulator proposes is one in which the willingness to pay for the marginal units to be purchased by a pair of households, say 1 and 2, differ. Imagine that household 1's willingness to pay for the marginal unit it is to consume exceeds that of household 2. Total wealth could be increased by a slight change in the regulator's plan: reduce household 2's consumption of X by one unit and raise household 1's consumption by one unit. No additional resources would be involved in this reassignment; but total wealth of households would increase, because household willingnesses to pay are measured in terms of wealth. So, we have proved that the efficient plan involves equality in the marginal willingness to pay among all households. A similar argument shows that the efficient plan also has the property that each household's marginal willingness to pay equals each firm's marginal cost of production. But the regulator would want to ensure that the total quantity produced equals the total quantity consumed. (Wealth would be wasted if total production exceeded total consumption; and the whole purpose of the planner would be frustrated if total production fell short of total consumption.) It is simple to confirm that there is a unique plan satisfying each of the above requirements.

Let the common value of the marginal costs of production and the marginal willingnesses to pay be P. The regulator could implement the efficient plan by setting the price of X at P and requiring that households and firms transact on the basis of P. That P is, of course, the P_E of Figure 2. This completes the proof.

Although highly abstract, what I have sketched here was the basis of a far reaching debate that took place among economists during the 1930s: markets versus central planning. Advocates of the institution of central planning, such as Oscar Lange and Abba Lerner, argued that an enlightened planner could help to realize all the virtues of markets while avoiding the weaknesses of actual markets, such as lapses from competition. The term *market socialism* has been associated with the Lange-Lerner vision. Advocates of markets, such as Friedrich von Hayek, argued, on the other hand, that the equivalence in the *outcomes* achieved doesn't amount to an equivalence in the amounts of *information* required in the two systems for achieving the desired outcome. Von Hayek observed that enlightenment on the part of the central planner in market socialism amounts also to omniscience. If the planner is to implement the efficient outcome, he or she needs to know each household's demand curve and each firm's supply curve. That's a lot of information. How is the planner to obtain it? Perhaps by sending polite questionnaires to households and firms. But why should respondents tell the truth about themselves and their circumstances? Even if ingenious mechanisms could be devised for eliciting that information, there are costs involved in collating and transmitting the information. Markets are far more parsimonious in the use of information.

One can argue though that the job of the planner shouldn't be to mimic the market, but to select policy weapons (such as taxes and subsidies) that require less information than is available to an omniscient being.

Even with limited knowledge, a planner could help to bring about states of affairs that are superior to those brought about by unbridled markets (Chapter 8).

Interdependent Markets

Marshall's famous demand and supply curves mislead in one important way. Figure 2 could lead one to think that in an ideal market, the equilibrium price of X is unique. We confirmed that it is unique (it was P_E), but we had assumed the prices of all other goods and services in the economy to be given. If those prices were to be different, the demand and supply curves of X would be different, which in turn would imply that the equilibrium price would be different. But all those other prices depend on demand and supply in their respective markets. As markets are interdependent, we should study them together, not one by one, separately.

We continue to assume that transactions are verifiable, as is the quality of the goods produced, sold, and bought. In other words, ideal markets don't suffer from problems of adverse selection and moral hazard. Moreover, markets open *now* for *every* commodity, including primary factors of production, intermediate goods, and final consumption goods. Most commodities would be future goods, which means that contracts over their purchases and sales are signed in *forward* markets. Contracts in forward markets involve agreements over purchases and sales today for delivery at specified future dates. Saving and investing for the future and borrowing from the future would take place in those markets. Many of the commodities would be contingent goods. Contracts over their purchases and sales would be signed in *contingent* markets. Contracts in contingent markets involve agreements over their purchases and sales today for delivery at specified future dates, *if and only if* certain contingencies arise.

The purchase and sale of insurance would take place in contingent markets. There is uncertainty about future events, but in contingent markets people are able to purchase or sell goods and services at quoted prices that are tied to each and every eventuality. As payments have to be made now, no one faces uncertainty over their budget, nor do firms face any uncertainty over their profits.

What is the point of studying a world in which there is a market for every conceivable good? There are three reasons. First, studying it enables us to appreciate that certain features of economic life in the world we live in arise because of missing markets (such as bankruptcy; performance-related pay; limits imposed on you by firms on the amount of insurance or credit you can purchase even if you have the resources to buy more; unemployment). Second, we can gauge how much societies lose from the fact that there are missing markets. And third, we can explore policies and institutions that could partially compensate for the absence of certain markets. That is why it makes sense to begin the study of interdependent markets in our world by investigating a world where there is a competitive market for every commodity.

We are studying a private ownership economy here. Firms are owned by households. Firms' profits are distributed to households on the basis of the shares they own. Each household has a legal right also to a set of commodities (their human capital). Therefore, for any given set of prices, each household is able to compute its wealth. Households are price-takers and are obliged to purchase goods and services they can afford: their total expenditure must not exceed their wealth. Firms are price-takers and choose their production outlays so as to maximize their profits, which in the present context means the capitalized value of the flow of profits. (Traders can be thought of as firms too. Their purchases can be regarded as "production" inputs, their sales as outputs.) A *market equilibrium*—economists call it a *competitive equilibrium*—is a set of prices quoted today for each and every commodity, such that the total demand for each equals its total supply. In equilibrium the information households and firms need to have in order to participate effectively is parsimonious. A household needs to know its own "mind," its endowment of goods and services, and the equilibrium prices—nothing else. Similarly, a firm needs only to know the technology available to it, the prices it has to pay for its inputs in production, and the prices of whatever it produces—nothing else. Equilibrium prices coordinate the production and allocation of all goods and services (who produces what and who consumes what).

Are there circumstances in which an equilibrium exists? Economists' search for an answer to the question has a history, dating back to the nineteenth century. The definitive answer was provided in the early 1950s, when several economists identified conditions (on households' and firms' characteristics) under which a competitive equilibrium exists. It was also shown that there is a close, but subtle, connection between the notion of a competitive equilibrium and that of an equilibrium agreement in a community (Chapters 2–3).

Excepting under very special circumstances, a competitive equilibrium is not unique. It isn't unique for much the same sort of reason as why equilibrium outcomes in communities are not unique (Chapter 2). Agreements in communities are mutually enforced by the use of social norms. The existence of more than one communitarian equilibrium reflects the fact that there is usually more than one set of self-confirming beliefs that people can harbor about one another's intentions. In ideal markets, agreements between buyers and sellers are enforced by the state exercising the rule of law. The existence of more than one competitive equilibrium reflects the fact that there is usually more than one set of prices at which demands for goods and services equal their supplies. Beliefs in communities and prices in markets are emergent features in two very different types of institutions. In Chapter 2, I explained the sense in which we don't yet have a satisfactory understanding of how beliefs form. You shouldn't be surprised that we don't yet have a satisfactory understanding of how prices would emerge in ideal markets.

The Efficiency of Ideal Markets

Even though equilibrium in a market economy isn't unique, every competitive equilibrium is "efficient." As we are now studying all the markets together, the notion of efficiency is not as simple as in the market for a single commodity (X), but it can be stated in words.

By an *allocation* of goods and services we mean a complete specification of who produces what and who consumes what. We say that an allocation is *feasible* if, given the economy's endowments of assets, it can in principle be created in the economy. Let α be a feasible allocation. We say that α is *efficient* if there is no feasible allocation that *all* households would choose over α. The concept was introduced by the economist-sociologist Vilfredo Pareto, which is why efficiency in the above sense is widely known as *Pareto-efficiency*. It can be shown that a competitive equilibrium is Pareto-efficient.

As with households, so with nations. If there were no restrictions in international trade, competitive equilibria of the world economy would be Pareto-efficient. Details aside, this is at the heart of the theoretical case for free trade.

Market Failure

Just as communities can fail to advance the interests of their members, markets can fail to allocate resources well. What households are able to achieve even in ideal markets depends on what they bring to the market place. Presumably, some households would be poorly endowed in goods and services, others richly so. Those endowments are inheritances from the past and they influence the outcome in the market place. Even though market allocations in competitive equilibrium are Pareto-efficient, they aren't necessarily equitable or just. It shouldn't be surprising that Pareto-efficiency is silent on distributive justice. Equity and efficiency are different ethical properties of allocations. An allocation of goods and services where one self-regarding household is assigned everything is Pareto-efficient, whereas an allocation in which households have equal shares is more equal. An allocation could be at once egalitarian and not be Pareto-efficient; it could be both egalitarian and Pareto-efficient; and there are allocations that are neither egalitarian nor Pareto-efficient. It is this sort of reasoning, though abstract and technical, that lies at the heart of a widely accepted role for government (Chapter 8): devising and implementing policies that would be expected to bring about outcomes that are Pareto-efficient (for practical purposes, read "tolerably non-wasteful") and egalitarian (for practical purposes, read "free of hunger, ill-health, and illiteracy").

Even if we were to leave distributional issues aside, markets don't operate ideally in the world we know. Why? Three reasons stand out. First, as the production of public goods is vulnerable to the free-riding problem, markets are less than effective in supplying them. That said, there are deeper problems than "free-riding" in the case of public goods.

Take the rule of law, which is a public good. In the absence of the rule of law markets couldn't function (Chapter 2), which means that it would be absurd to allow it to be a marketable commodity. There are also cases involving environmental services (Chapter 7), where market transactions create externalities that can't be eliminated no matter how audaciously the state tries to redefine private property rights.

Monopoly

The second reason is that in some industries there is a single producer (monopoly) or at best only a few producers (oligopoly). Firms in an ideal market don't have anything left over after every production input has been paid for (wages, salaries, raw materials, repair and maintenance, charges imputed to machinery and equipment, interest payments on loans, and so on). Because a monopolist doesn't face competition from other firms, it's able to charge a price higher than P_E (Figure 2) and enjoy a profit.

Monopolists have a bad press in consequence. However, we need monopolists because profits from sales are the incentives firms must have if they are to spend resources in research and development (R&D), so as to create new products and invent cheaper ways of producing old products (which is a good thing). Moreover, monopolists try to maintain their leading position by engaging in R&D, thereby forestalling entry by rivals (a not-so-good thing). Unless they are curbed, though, monopolists would wish to more than just recoup those R&D expenses. In rich countries antitrust laws have been legislated so as to prevent firms from doing that.

Monopolies are a necessary evil for another reason. There are commodities whose cost of production per unit produced declines with output. Economists call this phenomenon *economies of scale.*

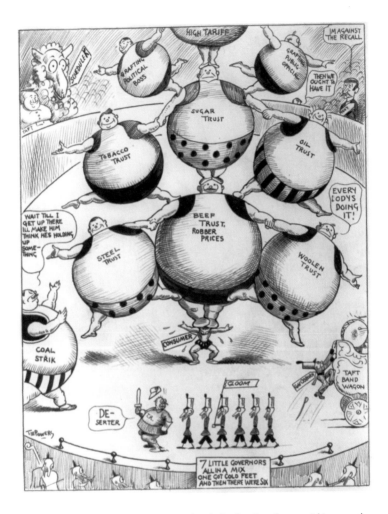

A 1912 cartoon attacks the power of monopolies, depicted as circus figures weighing upon the shoulders of the American consumer. Anti-trust laws have been instituted in many countries to prevent monopolies from gaining too much power.

In a 2004 scene from Desta's world, women sell seeds in an open-air market in Ethiopia's northeast Tigrea region, which is still recovering from the devastating 1984–5 famine that killed one million people.

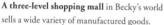

A three-level shopping mall in Becky's world sells a wide variety of manufactured goods.

Infrastructure (road networks, rail tracks, power, sewage systems) provides examples. Communities can't afford to produce them because communities are small. In contrast, the market would produce them if its reach was large enough and the costs of collecting fees from users was small enough. A firm that produces infrastructure has to be large in order to enjoy low production costs. So private producers of infrastructure are often monopolies, or at best oligopolies. As Becky's world has grown richer and the reach of the market has widened, societies there have increasingly relied on private firms to supply infrastructure even as they have directed their governments to regulate producers in order that they don't earn monopoly profits. Transport networks are a case in point. Of course, when households make use of such infrastructure as a modern sewage system, they confer benefits on others (positive externalities), which may be why in Becky's world the local government usually provides the service. In Desta's world infrastructure, such as durable roads, are often absent because of a vicious causal circle: in the absence of a reliable network of roads, markets can't extend their reach; in the absence of markets, households are unable to engage in anonymous transactions; and because government corruption is rampant in the construction sector, roads that would last don't get built; so households remain in poverty.

Macroeconomic Fluctuations

The third reason markets are far from ideal arises from a fact we noted earlier, that markets can support transactions only when transactions are verifiable. Markets for different qualities of a product, for example, can form only if quality can be verified. Moral hazard and adverse selection prevent markets from being formed, which is why few forward and contingent markets exist in the world we know. Households and firms are obliged to make decisions on the basis of the current value of their assets, the spot prices they face for goods and services, and the expectations they harbor about the prices (including wages) they will face when spot markets form in the future. As expectations can be held together by their own bootstraps, there can be more than one set of self-confirming expectations in the short run. Some lead to a reasonable utilization of the economy's productive capacity, others to slumps.

Analyses of slumps are the stuff of *macroeconomics*, which is concerned with the study of (national) economies considered in aggregate terms (Chapter 1). Historically, though, macroeconomics as a subject was devised to study *short-run* fluctuations in aggregate economic activity as measured in terms of such indices as output (GDP), employment, and the price level (which is the level of commodity prices, in the aggregate, in terms of money).

What are those fluctuations? Consider that since World War II, Becky's world has enjoyed improvements in the standard of living in a fairly uninterrupted way (Chapter 1). But GDP has been periodically less than potential GDP, which is the aggregate output the economy would have produced if all the installed machinery, equipment, and all the available labor force at the time were to have been employed. During the Great Depression of the 1930s, the economic slump in Europe and the US was so deep that not only did factories and equipment lie idle, some 25–30% of the labor force couldn't find a job in the market place. What is the explanation behind slumps and the labor unemployment that can go with them?

Depression-era "hunger marchers" advance on Washington, D.C., in 1931, to demand unemployment insurance and other social programs to protect workers. With unemployment at record levels, social unrest also increased dramatically, forcing government and business to make many concessions demanded by workers.

Economists have offered many explanations. They are often seen as reflecting different schools of thought: Keynesian, new-Keynesian, Classical, new-Classical, Real Business Cycle theories, and so on; which is as it should be, because it would be most odd if all slumps were the same. Throughout the 1990s that post-war economic miracle, Japan, experienced an economic slump that has only now begun to show signs of ending. Over the past decade the official unemployment rate in France and that other post-war economic miracle, Germany, has been about 10%, while in the UK it has been 4–5%. The unemployment rate in the US has been in the region of 6% for a number of years. As you might expect, the countries differ in regard to labor laws, taxation, unemployment benefits, and social security; and Germany reunified at the beginning of the 1990s. Countries in Becky's world differ also in the mundane matter of what criteria to use for registering someone as unemployed. We should be astonished if one account could cover all slumps. Limitations of space forbid that we discuss macroeconomic fluctuations and the government's potential role in smoothing them at a high level of economic activity. That's a subject deserving of its own very short introduction. Nevertheless, it will be instructive to sketch a model that shows how that ubiquitous mental state, *expectations*, can play a role in bringing about slumps in the market place.

So consider a situation where, for one reason or other (perhaps because of rumors: Chapter 2), producers believe demand for their products will be low. It would then be in each producer's interest to cut back production, run down inventories, and reduce the demand for labor. If the supply of labor is constant, there would be excess labor in the market place. If adjustments occur quickly, wages would fall. But if wages fall, then incomes fall, which then leads to a decline in the demand for goods and services at the level of prices with which we began our account. That decline in turn causes the price level to fall. But lower prices lead employers to lower their demand for labor, so that the original short-run expectations on the part of employers are confirmed. To put it another way, when producers expect prices and wages to move together, aggregate output doesn't respond much to a change in the price level. Each producer heaves a sigh of relief that he hadn't made a mistake in his (short-run) economic forecast, but would be justifiably anxious that times were bad.

In contrast, suppose for one reason or other producers believe demand for their products will be high. Then it would be in each producer's interest to maintain (even raise) production and build up inventories. An analogous piece of reasoning suggests that such beliefs could be self-confirming in the short run. Each producer would heave a sigh of relief that he hadn't made a mistake in his economic forecast, and would feel justifiably jubilant that times were good.

Problems are exacerbated if prices or wages are sticky. The economist Joseph Stiglitz has shown that the phenomena of moral hazard and adverse selection in the labor market can create conditions where real wages are rigid in the downward direction. If the real wage for a particular type of work is downwardly rigid and the demand for workers at that wage is less than the supply, obviously some workers will fail to get hired. Those who are fortunate to be hired are better off than those who are rejected. Economists call that state of affairs *involuntary unemployment*, to distinguish the situation from one where, say, someone is temporarily unemployed because he is searching for a better job than the one he had earlier. That wage rigidity will not bite if producers, buoyed by high expectations, demand lots of labor, which is why exuberant expectations can lift an economy by their own bootstraps to full employment.

John Maynard Keynes, Michal Kalecki, and Bertil Ohlin were prominent among those economists who, in the 1930s, recommended active government engagement for reviving depressed economies. Their ideas were extended greatly by the economists James Meade, Paul Samuelson, and James Tobin, among others. One way to interpret the need for fiscal and monetary policies during severe slumps (taxes and subsidies, public investment, interest rates, credit facilities) is that they help to change the expectations people hold about the future. But finding the right combination of public policies can be a nightmare: different slumps require different palliatives, which is why macroeconomic stabilization continues to be a controversial subject.

FIVE

Science and Technology as Institutions

•

INSTITUTIONS ARE PUBLIC GOODS. The problem facing a society is to unearth what combination is likely to work best for it. In the rest of this book we explore how institutions interact with one another. To see what issues are involved, it will pay to begin by studying the institutions that have been created to produce a commodity that any reader of books would find interesting: *knowledge*.

Knowledge is a public good *par excellence*. It is non-rivalrous in use (when someone applies the calculus to a problem, no one else is prevented from applying the calculus to his or her problems). Unless the producer of a piece of knowledge is secretive, it is also non-excludable. Knowledge is a durable commodity, in that the same piece of knowledge can be used over and over again. If someone was to invent the wheel

Stacks of patent paperwork line the shelves of the US Patent Office c. 1910–20. Knowledge is a commodity, and technological and scientific breakthroughs are valuable "goods" that can be protected by patent law.

today, we would observe that he had merely "reinvented the wheel"; he wouldn't contribute anything of value. Moreover, as no additional cost is involved when someone dips into a piece of knowledge, he shouldn't be charged for it.

These observations are truisms today, but they raise a problem. If knowledge is freely available to all, the only way discoverers and inventors could obtain a return on their efforts would be by being secretive or by earning profits from the head start they have with their ideas. Which means that the private incentives to produce knowledge would be low. The trick is to find more reliable ways to reward people who discover and invent.

In using the terms *discoverers* and *inventors*, I don't mean to restrict the use of the word *knowledge* to the products of science and technology; I want to include innovations in the arts, crafts, music, and literature. Nevertheless, in offering an account of the two overlapping institutions that have emerged in the modern era for producing knowledge, I shall rely on examples drawn from science and technology, conventionally defined. Along the way, we will discover that our analysis applies also to other forms of creative work.

By scientific and technological knowledge I mean, roughly speaking, what the classical Greeks meant by them, namely, *episteme* (speculative, theoretical, or abstract knowledge) and *techne* (art or practical knowledge), respectively. As far as I can tell, Aristotle regarded it impolite to discuss *techne*, even to enumerate achievements in that sphere. His discourses focused on *episteme*. In contrast, modern economists have attended to *techne*, which is evident from our frequent use of the term *technological progress* when we offer reasons for continued economic growth in Becky's world (Chapter 1).

Research and development (R&D) are inputs in the production of knowledge. Publicly funded R&D is the Wicksell-Samuelson solution (Chapter 2) to the problem of incentives in knowledge production. For reasons that will become clear presently, I shall call the institution of publicly funded R&D, *Science* (with uppercase S). For concreteness, the agency that funds R&D will be taken to be the state, even though private foundations and large corporations in Becky's world augment the resources that flow into Science from the state.

So that the knowledge that is produced with public funds is freely available to all, employment contracts include the condition that discoveries and inventions are to be disclosed publicly. But knowledge often involves technical material. How is the state to prevent quacks and charlatans from muddying the enterprise? Modern societies have solved this adverse selection problem by insisting that public disclosure involves publication in peer-reviewed journals. Vetting by peers greatly reduces a problem society faces, namely, its inability to distinguish good products from bad products.

But there are further problems in Science. As a good deal of creative work is conducted in the head and success in R&D is chancy, it isn't possible to verify whether someone has complied with the agreement to work hard. How is the paymaster to know that scientists are thinking, not daydreaming? After all, even lazy scientists could claim that they were unlucky, not lazy. Society therefore faces a moral hazard, implying that payment should not be based on time or effort. An alternative is a fixed payment for practicing science, but that too has a problem. If scientists could collect the fee irrespective of whether they produced anything of interest, the incentive to work hard would be blunted; which is yet another moral hazard. If each of these hazards is to be reduced, payment has to be based in some way on performance. Such forms of payment are called *piece rate*. In the present context, *piece rate* means payment on the basis of the quality of the product of R&D.

For reasons similar to the ones I have just enumerated, piece rates used to be a commonplace for casual labor in agricultural harvest. Today, machines set the pace, which means that human effort is verifiable. That is why piece rates have become less common even in agriculture. But performance bonuses, often in the form of stock options, are today a commonplace in large corporations, for reasons of the moral hazards facing shareholders (Chapter 6). In the knowledge sector, a special version of piece rate payment is alive and well and has played an enormously significant role in the economic transformations that have led to Becky's world.

In order to understand the version of piece rates prevalent in Science, let us recall that a piece of knowledge need not be produced more than once. If we were to interpret this literally, it would mean that those who produce a piece of knowledge after it has already been made public by someone else contribute nothing of value. That in turn implies that only the first with a discovery or invention should be rewarded. So as to encourage scientists to make fruitful discoveries, the payment schedule also needs to have the feature that, the better the discovery, the bigger is the reward. The idea therefore is to transform research into *contests*.

It can be argued that, in order to encourage entry into scientific contests, losers ought to be rewarded too. The problem is that losers could make inflated claims about their own progress once the winner discloses his or her finding. This possibility would create another moral hazard for the paymaster. The scheme that avoids each of these problems and has been adopted by Science is the *rule of priority*. Under that rule, the winner takes all that the paymaster has on offer. Science doesn't pay runners-up.

What I have just written isn't literally true of course. First, scientists are inevitably a garrulous lot, which means that colleagues usually know roughly how far behind the winner the losers were at the time the discovery was made public. Second, no two scientists follow exactly the same trail, which means that losers also produce material of interest. So, losers are rewarded, too. The "winner takes all" version of the rule of priority is simply a stylized way of saying that in Science, winners are rewarded disproportionately.

The rule of priority is ingenious, in that it elicits public disclosure of new findings by creating a private asset from the very moment a scientist relinquishes exclusive possession of the discovery. In Science, priority *is* the prize. In the words of the biologist Peter Medawar, it awards *moral* possession of discoveries to winners, even though no one obtains legal possession of them.

But there are problems with the rule of priority. It places all the risks that are inevitable in R&D firmly on the shoulders of scientists. This can't be an efficient system if scientists, like lesser mortals, are risk-averse. It would seem, after all, that in order to encourage entry into Science, scientists should be paid something whether or not they are successful in the contests they choose to enter. It is in this light that Kenneth Arrow's remark, that "the complementarity between teaching and research is, from the point of view of the economy, something of a lucky accident," assumes its full significance. That "complementarity" explains why so many scientists are employed in universities, and it explains why in recent centuries universities have been the place where some of the greatest advances in science have been made. Tenure in university appointments, a much debated feature of employment contracts, is a way society ties its hands not to interfere when a scientist has reasons to follow one research lead rather than another and other people have reasons to disagree with the scientist.

Although the reasoning I have deployed in arriving at the rule of priority draws on the language of modern economics, the rule itself became established much earlier than my discipline. (Societies are usually a lot cleverer than social thinkers.) The Royal Society of London (chartered in 1662) and similar Academies in Paris, Rome, and Berlin were established in order to facilitate the exchange of scientific knowledge and to confirm new discoveries and inventions. Those Academies also legitimized the rule of priority, administered it, and became the arena for struggles over conflicting claims to priority. The dispute between Newton and Leibnitz over moral possession of the calculus is only the most famous example.

But neither the rule of priority nor the Academies appeared in a vacuum. The economic historian Paul A. David has traced their origins to a problem rulers in the late Renaissance Italy faced increasingly: how to choose men of science who would adorn their courts. No doubt the evolution of institutions doesn't follow the dictates of analytical reasoning, but it is analytical reasoning that explains what evolutions amount to. Even the notion of moral ownership of creative works predates the Academies. For example, it was common practice among bards in medieval India to refer to themselves in their poems by name in the third person. By doing that, the poet left a signature on his creation (mostly they were men)—the better the poet, the greater his fame, the larger his audiences, and so, the greater his pecuniary benefits. Scribes, philosophers, and scholars in Eurasia had practiced the open transfer of knowledge even earlier. The anthropologist, Jack Goody, has uncovered the ingenious ways in which creators even in pre-literate societies left markers on their works so as to be remembered. But those earlier practices were haphazard. What the rule of priority did was to put the stamp of an institutional imprimatur on creative works.

There are limitations to Science. An exclusive dependence on the public purse to finance R&D is problematic, because knowledge has two further properties: no one truly knows what the commodity to be produced is until it has been produced; nor does anyone really know in advance how to produce it. Of course, experts are likely to have a better idea than others of which problems are solvable, by what means. If society wants to ensure that a wide portfolio of scientific and technological problems is on the table, it ought to encourage R&D activity not only in Science, but also in a parallel institution, where discoveries and inventions are privatized. Let us call that institution *Technology* (with an upper case T).

One way to keep knowledge from being used by others is to keep it secret. In earlier times practitioners of alchemy, witchcraft, magic, and the material crafts (glass-making, metallurgy, the manufacture of precision instruments), and experts at solving complex accounting problems for merchants and businessmen (for example, the cossists of sixteenth-century Germany) kept their knowledge and skills secret. In the age of maritime discoveries, maps of trade routes were carefully guarded. Holders of secrets were able to earn profits from their knowledge, which is why secrecy was practiced mostly over *techne*. But secrecy isn't reliable. Reverse engineering, to use a modern term,

Before the protection of patent law, many industries maintained their advantage through secrecy, with craftsmen carefully guarding trade practices. This 1556 woodcut from *De re metallica* (*On the Nature of Metals*) depicts four German metal workers, each responsible for a different task in the manufacturing process.

is a danger in the crafts, as is the possibility that rivals will make the same inventions. Monopoly rights to knowledge, or *patents*, is a remedy for that problem. The patent system—and relatedly, *copyright* for images and expressions—allows people to disclose their findings without obliging them to share the profits from those findings. It is a legal means of making a piece of knowledge an excludable commodity. The system offers a private reward for disclosure and makes the award on the basis of priority of disclosure. Like the rule of priority in Science, the patent system encourages contests in Technology.

The systematic use of patents began in Venice in 1474, when the Republic promised privileges of ten years to inventors of new arts and machines. But the forerunner of present day patent laws was the English Statute of Monopolies in 1623. This enunciated the general principle that only the "first and true" inventor of a new manufacture should be granted a monopoly patent—in the case of the 1623 statute, for a period of fourteen years. Even the forerunners of modern patent laws made it impossible to patent a "fact of nature," which is why it is customary to regard patents as belonging to the realm of *techne*. But recent litigations over patents in biotechnology have shown that it isn't always easy to agree on what is a fact of nature.

Let me sum up in the language that was developed in earlier chapters: behavior in Technology is market-driven and thus enforced by the *law*; whereas in Science, behavior is community-ridden and thus enforced by *norms*. Both institutions produce knowledge; but in the former, it is regarded as a private good, whereas in the latter, it is viewed as a public good. The incentives in Science and Technology differ in ways that encourage scientists and technologists to regard their products in accordance with the mores of the institution to which they belong. It should then be no surprise that the character of what is produced also differs. The traditional distinction between Science and Technology, which sees the former as being concerned with basic research (whose output is an input in the production of further knowledge) and the latter with applied research (whose output is an input in the production of goods and services), interprets the two in terms of differences in their products. The viewpoint being advanced here, of regarding Science and Technology as institutions, seems to be me to be deeper. It helps to explain *why* their outputs would be expected to differ.

Today, we take it for granted that Science has in place incentives for scientists to disclose their findings. But the emergence of the social contrivances that embody those incentives was not inevitable. Nor did they emerge easily, for it required the collective efforts of scientists and their patrons. The role of Academies in subjecting claims to independent scrutiny, in adjudicating between rival claims for priority and in overseeing the quality of those who enter Science, has been substantial. Peer-group esteem, medals, and scrolls, being the currency in which scientists are rewarded, are remarkable innovations because they don't involve too many resources. In order that those social contrivances are effective, a good part of a scientist's education involves developing a taste for non-pecuniary rewards. That taste has enabled Science to produce knowledge on the cheap. Increasingly though, the taste for those social contrivances has to compete against the pecuniary rewards available in Technology. If the pecuniary rewards increase—and they have increased greatly in recent years—the taste for the mores in Science becomes more and more of a luxury to the research worker. Science embodies a set of cultural values in need of constant protection from the threat posed by its rival, Technology. That threat has proved to be so real, that in recent decades the two institutions have begun to blur into each other. Scientists increasingly behave like technologists, while technologists enjoy both the pecuniary rewards of Technology and the medals and scrolls that Science has to offer.

Despite the tensions, Science and Technology continue to progress in Becky's world. Today, expenditure on R&D amounts to 2.5% of the GDP of rich nations, while the corresponding figure in poor nations is a good deal less than 1%. Given that the GDP of rich nations is six times that of poor nations, we shouldn't be surprised that the bulk of scientific and technological advances are taking place in Becky's world, nor that Desta's world manages at best to be a limited user of those advances. And I haven't even mentioned the relative expenditures on education in the two worlds.

The institutional innovations in Science and Technology that I have just sketched, all too briefly, took place in Europe and emerged during the period historians refer to as the Age of Enlightenment. The latter term can grate if it is interpreted in an epistemological sense. And it does grate among intellectuals, because that's how the term is usually interpreted. They bristle at the suggestion that the analytic-empirical basis of knowledge—which is what both Science and Technology are built on—is a European invention. And they ask: "what about those civilizations at earlier times, in other places, that nurtured scholars who made enduring contributions to knowledge?"

Let it be acknowledged, once and for all, that the analytic-empirical basis isn't an invention of Becky's world, and that the mystical-revelatory route to the acquisition of knowledge isn't restricted to Desta's world. Every society that I am even dimly familiar with has fielded both, often at the same time. Which may explain why people today from all parts of the globe are able to practice Science and Technology with ease when given half a chance; their "cultural" background doesn't seem to be an intellectual bottleneck. Brandishing texts to show that scientific and technological progress was made in Desta's world at a time when Becky's was covered in darkness doesn't advance knowledge, it merely reiterates the commonplace. What Europe achieved during the Age of Enlightenment was far more remarkable than a revolution in epistemology, in that no place had managed to do it before. It created institutions that enabled the production, dissemination, and use of knowledge—in effect, the entire knowledge industry—to be transferred from *small elites* to the *public at large*, a transfer that so sharpened the analytic-empirical mode of reasoning that it became routine. That achievement explains a good deal of the macroeconomic statistics I reported in Chapter 1.

SIX

Households and Firms

●

COMMUNITIES AND MARKETS ARE overarching institutions. People operate in them not only directly, but also through a number of smaller institutions, of which households and business enterprises are the most prominent. In exploring these institutions it will pay to ask what it is that people seek to achieve through them. Admittedly, the household is so deeply rooted in humankind that it may seem odd to enquire after its economic purpose. But even that most ubiquitous of institutions has been known to undergo changes in response to resource scarcities. I shall not elaborate on the more obvious roles households and business enterprises play in enabling people to survive and, if they have coordinated well with one another and have been lucky, even to prosper. Instead, we will study some of their more distinctive features so as to get a better understanding of the huge differences between Becky's and Desta's lives.

The nuclear family is the most common household found in the United States, where extended families are no longer the norm. This Depression-era family was photographed in 1937, in Greenbelt, Maryland.

Households

Among sedentary communities, the family is the institution that has traditionally harbored the strongest personal ties. Economists and statisticians find it useful to work with a more contemporary notion—the *household*—which is a smaller unit than the family. The household is usually taken to mean a unit of housekeeping or consumption. Its members eat meals together or share meals that are derived from a common stock of food.

We assume that parents wish to protect and promote household well-being, by which I mean the well-beings of its members, taken together. But the parents may have different notions of what "taken together" means. In Desta's world, where the extended family influences household decisions, not only do the parents matter, grandparents (even the wider network of kin) also influence household decisions.

Social scientists have discovered that the allocation of basic needs—leisure, food, health care, and education—are distributed unequally within households in Desta's world. Some of those inequities are borne out of sheer necessity. Consider the allocation of food. About 60–75% of the daily energy intake of a person in nutritional balance goes toward maintenance (blood circulation, brain activity, tissue repair, metabolism, and so forth), while the remaining 25–40% is spent in discretionary activities (work and leisure). The 60–75% is rather like a "fixed" need: over the long run people need it as a minimum no matter what they do. We should therefore expect food to be distributed unequally in very poor households, even though it would have been distributed equally in those same households had they been rich. To see why, suppose the energy requirement for daily maintenance is 1,500 kilocalories (kcal). Consider a household of four that has access only to 5,000 kcal. Equal sharing would mean that no one would have sufficient energy to spare. Sharing food unequally enables the most productive member to work and increase the chances that the household's future will be better. On the other hand, if the household had access to a lot more than 6,000 kcal, it would be able to share food equally without jeopardizing its future. When food is very scarce, the younger and weaker members of Desta's household are given less to eat than the others, even after allowance is made for differences in their age. In good times, though, Desta's parents can afford to be egalitarian. In contrast, Becky's household can always afford enough food. Her parents allocate food equally every day—again, allowing for differences in nutritional needs.

Gender Inequalities

The considerations I have just outlined can't on their own explain the persistence and magnitude of household inequalities in the poor world. In a notable article, the demographer Pravin Visaria observed that the female–male ratio in India had shown a decline since the Indian Census of 1901; worse, it has been considerably less than 1. According to the most recent census, there are 93 women to every 100 men in India. In the rich world today, the ratio is 106 to 100. In answering a question the epidemiologist Lincoln Chen posed in response to Visaria's finding, namely, "Where have the women gone?," he and his collaborators collected gender-based mortality and anthropometric statistics from villages in the Indian sub-continent and discovered male bias in the allocation of food and health care in poor households. The suspicion is that parents not only practice female infanticide, but also withhold postnatal health care so as to reduce the number of girls in the household.

Health discrimination against girls isn't limited to the Indian sub-continent; it exists in China, too. When social norms insist that parents pay crippling dowries and that sons look after their elderly parents, a preference for male children is inevitable among poor households. However, if we suppose that mothers are likely to have greater empathy than fathers have with daughters, we should expect discrimination against female children over food and health care to be less in households where women are educated, or have access to paid employment, or control the household budget, other things being equal. There is evidence that this is so, both in the Indian sub-continent and in sub-Saharan Africa.

The ratio of females to males in sub-Saharan Africa is 102 to 100, which means the female–male imbalance in India isn't exclusively a reflection of poverty. The demographer Esther Boserup observed that women have a prominent role in agriculture involving hoe farming (such as in sub-Saharan Africa), in contrast to regions (such as the Indian sub-continent) where plow farming is predominant. Boserup drew a connection between the technology of food cultivation and the position of women. Gender discrimination in the Indian sub-continent varies across ecological zones. Women are much involved in paddy cultivation, where manual dexterity, not so much brawn, is needed. Women are less involved in wheat cultivation, where brawn is an essential input (working with the plow requires physical strength). In India the female–male ratio is higher in rice producing states (they are in the south and east) than in wheat producing states (they are, in the main, in the north).

Gender imbalances in health within households in the poor world are related to fertility choice. Since women bear the far greater cost in bearing and rearing children, we should expect men to desire more children than women. On the other hand, if women are economically more vulnerable than men, they would desire more children than men because children offer an insurance against particularly bad circumstances. Either way, birth rates would be expected to be lower in societies where women are more empowered. Data on the status of women in Desta's world display an unmistakable pattern: high fertility, high rates of female illiteracy, low women's share of paid employment, and a high percentage of women working at home for no pay, go hand in hand.

Property Rights and Fertility

We have now studied two factors that shape fertility behavior: conformism and gender relations. The two together go some way toward explaining the striking differences in fertility rates between Becky's and Desta's worlds. But there are significant differences in fertility behavior between the Indian sub-continent and sub-Saharan Africa also, owing probably to differences in property rights in the two regions. (In recent decades fertility rates there have differed by about 2.) Parental costs of procreation are lower when the cost of rearing the child is shared among the kinship (another case of strong ties). In sub-Saharan Africa fosterage within the kinship is a commonplace. Children are not raised solely by their parents; the responsibility is more diffuse within the kinship group. Fosterage in the African context doesn't break ties between parents and children. The institution affords a form of mutual insurance protection. Because opportunities for saving are few in the low-productivity agricultural regions of sub-Saharan Africa, it may be that fosterage also enables households to smooth their consumption across time. In parts of West Africa up to half the children have been found to be living with kin at any given time. Nephews and nieces have the same rights of accommodation and support as do biological offspring. If the parents' share of the benefits from having children exceeds their share of the costs, the arrangement creates a free-rider problem. From the point of view of parents, taken as a collective, too many children would be produced in these circumstances.

In sub-Saharan Africa, communal land tenure within the lineage social structure has in the past offered further inducement for households to procreate. Large families are (or, at least were, until recently) rewarded by a greater share of land belonging to the lineage or clan. Communal land tenure and a strong kinship support system of children, taken together, are a source of reproductive externalities, stimulating fertility. In contrast, agricultural land is not held communally in the Indian

An extended family gathers in the village of Gabisi, Ghana. Large families are encouraged in sub-Saharan African communities.

sub-continent, which is probably a reflection of greater land scarcity there. Large family size leads to fragmentation of landholdings, which dampens the incentive to procreate.

Transaction Needs of Households
(1) INSURANCE

To insure oneself against a risk is to act in ways to reduce the risk. People do that by exchanging goods and services across uncertain contingencies, paying small sums no matter what (the premia) and receiving compensation in case of bad luck. Avoiding risk would seem to be a universal urge. If Desta's parents had a choice between $5,000 for certain and an even chance of either $4,000 or $6,000, they would choose the sure income. Although the mean income in the two alternatives is the same ($5,000), the latter involves risk while the former doesn't. But what if they were offered a choice between $5,000 for sure and an even chance of either $3,000 or $11,000? The latter option is risky, but its mean (or average) is $7,000 (namely, $(3,000 + 11,000)/2$), which is a lot higher than $5,000 dollars. Which option they would choose isn't clear. Risk-averse people do take risks, but only if those risks offer correspondingly higher expectations of income. In the present example, the lower value, $3,000, could compromise the household's future. In which case the risky option would be rejected. Similarly, people pay to lower the risks they face, but only if what they have to pay isn't too high.

Households in Desta's village have no access to insurance companies; nor does the government offer insurance against calamities. Villagers insure one another by practicing reciprocity (Chapter 2). The problem is that communities are able to offer individual households very little cushion against risks. When Desta's father's crops fail because the rains have let him down or because there has been an infestation of pests, the crops in neighboring fields don't do well either. Desta's household needs help precisely when others in their community need help. Similarly, when Desta's household has enjoyed a good harvest, other households have, too. In statistical language, agricultural risks within the village are "positively correlated." So, although communities are essential for survival in Desta's world, they are unable to offer households much opportunity to improve their lot. Because people can't insure themselves sufficiently against failure, they are reluctant to undertake activities offering a chance of huge success if there is also an accompanying chance of large failure. Desta's world has remained poor in part because they haven't created institutions that enable people to engage in productive, but risky activities.

As the insurance they are able to obtain against crop failure is very limited, households in Desta's village adopt additional risk-reducing strategies, such as diversifying their crops. Desta's parents plant maize, *teff*, and enset (an inferior crop), with the hope that even if maize were to fail one year, enset wouldn't let them down. That the local resource base in Desta's village is communally owned could well be in part due to a mutual desire to pool risks. Woodlands are spatially non-homogeneous ecosystems. In one year one group of plants bears fruit, in another year some other group does. If the woodland were divided into private parcels, each household would face a greater risk than it would under communal ownership. The reduction in individual household risks owing to communal ownership may be small, but as average incomes are very low, household benefits from communal ownership are large.

Many social practices in the poor world reflect the common desire to reduce risks. For example, patrilocal residence and patrilineality enable men to exploit the knowledge they have gained from childhood of the idiosyncrasies of their soil. Both practices are the established norm in most agrarian cultures that are based on the plow. Relatedly, the larger is the distance between a pair of villages, the smaller is the likely correlation between their agricultural outputs. We should expect rural households facing greater risks of crop failure to form marriage alliances with households in villages located at greater distances. There is scattered evidence of this as well.

Becky's parents, in contrast to Desta's, have access to an elaborate set of insurance markets that pool the risks of hundreds of thousands of households across the country (even the world, if the insurance company is a multinational). Moreover, the government comes to the rescue if there are uninsured emergencies (earthquakes, floods). This helps to reduce individual risks a lot more than Desta's parents are able to realize. Why? First, spatially distant risks are more likely to be unrelated to one another than risks nearby. Second, Becky's parents can pool their risk with many more households. With enough households and enough independence of risks from one another, mutual insurance can pretty well guarantee each household a low risk outcome. This is an implication of the famous Law of Large Numbers in probability theory. Bad luck experienced by one household is almost surely matched by good luck in another household living far away under different circumstances. What the Law of Large Numbers says is that if insurance firms are made to compete against one another, the premia that households would be charged would equal the sum of the average liability and the cost of administering insurance. Of course, those costs can be large, for they include not only the time and resources spent in the inevitable paperwork, but also the resources needed to screen out bad risks (protection of the insurance firms against adverse selection) and monitoring that due care has been taken by insurees against bad outcomes

New Orleans residents await rescue on a rooftop after Hurricane Katrina struck in 2005. The US government provides assistance to victims in the event of emergencies such as earthquakes or floods.

(protection against moral hazard). By being able to take advantage of the Law of Large Numbers, markets and the government, taken together, are far superior to communities, despite those administration costs. People are able to cover their risks to a remarkable degree in markets. Being able to do so, they are emboldened to accept ventures that are risky but offer high expected yields. This is one reason why Becky's world is now so rich.

(ii) Borrowing, Saving, and Investing

If you don't take out insurance, your income will depend heavily on whether you are lucky or unlucky. Purchasing insurance helps to reduce dependence on luck. The human desire to reduce that dependence is related to the equally common desire to smooth (that is, equalize) consumption across time. You don't want to feast and fast or experience booms and busts periodically; you want to eat and drink moderately every day, enjoy vacations on a regular basis, and so on. Of course, people do incur large expenditures at certain periods of their life, such as buying a home, paying children's school fees, celebrating marriages, and meeting funeral costs. The flow of income over a lifetime tends not to match expenditure needs. So, people look for ways to transfer expenditure across time. Mortgages, saving for children's education, and pensions help to do that. Becky's parents took out a mortgage on their house, because at the time of purchase they couldn't finance it without a loan. The resulting debt decreased their future consumption but enabled them to buy the house at the time they did. Becky's parents also pay into a pension fund, which transfers present consumption to their retired future. Desta's father joined the *iddir* in order to pay for funerals. Borrowing for current consumption transfers future consumption to the present; saving and investing achieve the reverse. Since capital assets are productive, a dollar invested today becomes something more than a dollar tomorrow. This is one reason why in Becky's world borrowing involves having to pay interest, saving in financial institutions means receiving interest, and investing in the stock market yields positive returns (hopefully!).

In order to formalize these ideas about market economies, let us ignore uncertainty and imagine that you can buy a piece of machinery—say from abroad—for $100,000, which, after annual costs have been met for labor, intermediate goods, maintenance and replacement of parts, and marketing, will yield you a net income of $5,000 every year. This means that if you buy the machinery, your investment will yield a return of 5% (5,000/100,000) a year. Imagine now that there are large numbers of investment opportunities. For you to purchase the machinery and put it to work, it must be that no available investment opportunity yields a return greater than 5% a year. Presumably there are lots of projects that yield less than 5% a year. Those you simply dismiss out of hand.

You happen to have lots of money (in fact, you are a bank!) and someone comes to you for a loan of $100,000 to finance the purchase of a home. You should charge the borrower an interest rate of 5% on the capital you advance. Anything less and you would lose income (you would be better off investing in another one of those pieces of machinery or any other investment opportunity yielding 5% a year); anything more and a rival bank will attract the borrower by undercutting you with a lower interest rate. But you like to specialize as a banker. So you don't want to go into production yourself; rather, you lend money to entrepreneurs who wish to go into production. What interest rate do you charge those entrepreneurs? 5% of course. If you charge less, you will face an unlimited demand for loans; if you charge more, no one will come to you for a loan.

While competition determines the interest rates private banks can charge individuals and businesses, the US Federal Reserve, America's central bank, pursues monetary policy by controlling the interest rates charged on interbank loans.

A simple way to formulate the issues Becky's parents face when they deliberate over their consumption and saving decisions is to imagine that they regard themselves as members of a dynasty. This is another way of saying that Becky's parents are concerned not only with their own well-being and that of Becky and Sam, but also the well-being of their potential grandchildren, great grandchildren, and so on. They don't do that explicitly of course. Becky's parents take only their children's well-being directly into account; but (and this is the point) they know that Becky and Sam, when they in turn come to make their consumption and saving decisions, will take into account the well-being of *their* children, that the grandchildren in turn will take into account the well-being of the great grandchildren, and so on, down the generations. Becky's parents make a considerable investment in their children's education; but they don't expect to be repaid for this, nor do they set aside funds for their grandchildren's education, for the latter are regarded as Becky's and Sam's future responsibilities. In Becky's world, resources are transferred from parents to children. Children are a direct source of parental well-being; they are not investment goods. Needless to say, expectations about future events play a huge role in these intergenerational deliberations.

There is evidence that people prefer to consume now rather than wait, other things being equal. This is a way of saying that we are impatient. It may be that we are so disposed because of the small chance that there will be no tomorrow for us, or it may be because we fear that the consumption prospect may not be available if we wait (recall the expression: "a bird in the hand is better than two in the bush"). Whatever the innate reason, impatience means that we discount future consumption simply because it is to appear in the future. But people also have a desire to equalize their consumption across time, other things being equal; which is another way of saying that we have less of a want for a marginal increase in consumption when consumption is already high than when consumption is low. However, neither impatience nor the desire for smoothing consumption squares with the fact that in Becky's world people have been growing richer and richer and consuming more and more over many decades, nor with the fact that they expect to continue doing so over the foreseeable future. Why didn't people save less in the past so as to smooth consumption? Equally, why don't Becky's parents raise their current consumption at the expense of some of their children's future consumption?

In order to find an explanation, we assume, realistically, that the rate of return on saving is greater than the rate at which people are impatient to consume now. For theoretical purposes we may as well then imagine that the rate of impatience is negligible and that the capital market offers a positive return on saving—say, 5% a year. Consider now a household that can afford a consumption level of $120,000 this year and $120,000 next year (which we write as ($120,000, $120,000)). As the rate of return on saving is 5% a year, the household can certainly also afford the prospect ($119,999, $120,001). The desire for equality of consumption over time means that the household regards ($120,000, $120,000) to be a bit more desirable than ($119,999, $120,001). So, if the household were asked to consume $119,999 worth of goods and services now, it would desire something in excess of $120,001 worth of goods and services next year as compensation. Is there a consumption prospect that the household can afford and that it regards to be more desirable than ($120,000, $120,000)? The answer is "yes." We can even say something more: the desire for smoothing and the prospect of a positive return on saving mean that of all those consumption prospects a household can afford, the one it would find most desirable would have consumption rising over time.

To prove that, it will help to define a new term. Let us call the percentage rate at which the household is willing to substitute this year's consumption for consumption next year the household's *consumption discount rate* between the two years. If that rate is r, the household requires $(1 + r)$ worth of additional consumption next year for a reduction in $1 worth of consumption this year. Which is another way of saying that an extra dollar's worth of consumption for the household next year is worth $1/(1 + r)$ of consumption this year (a reasoning we deployed in Chapter 2). The magnitude of r depends on the consumption prospect. For example, the consumption discount rate of a household facing the prospect ($120,000, $120,000) is *zero* (the household is not impatient, remember, and desires to smooth consumption over time, other things being equal); whereas the consumption discount rate of a household facing the prospect ($120,000, $125,000) is *positive* (the household is not impatient and desires to smooth consumption over time, other things being equal).

We can now state a general result, whose present form is due to the economist Irving Fisher and the mathematician-philosopher-economist Frank Ramsey: among all consumption prospects the household can afford, the most desirable is the one along which, at every date, the consumption discount rate equals the rate of return on saving. The proof is simple: if the consumption discount rate is less than the rate of return on saving, the household would wish to save a bit more now. But to save a bit more now is to consume a bit less today, and this tilts consumption more toward the future, which in turn raises the consumption discount rate. Alternatively, if the discount rate is greater than the rate of return on saving, the household would wish to save a bit less now. But to save a bit less is to consume a bit more now, and that tilts consumption more toward the present, which in turn lowers the consumption discount rate. We have therefore proved that the best consumption prospect is the one along which the household's consumption discount rate equals the rate of return on saving.

The desire for consumption smoothing and an absence of impatience mean that the household's consumption discount rate is positive only if consumption increases with time. This explains why the desire to smooth consumption over time translates into growing consumption in a productive economy. We can generalize the result further: if the rate of impatience to consume is less than the rate of return on saving, then a household that desires to smooth its consumption would save so as to enjoy increasing consumption over time.

For Desta's parents the calculations are very different. Their household is heavily constrained in its ability to transfer consumption across time because they have no access to capital markets. Admittedly, Desta's parents invest in their land (clearing weeds, leaving portions fallow, and so forth), but that's to prevent the productivity of land from declining. Moreover, the only way Desta's family is able to consume maize following each harvest is to store the produce. The cruel fact is, though, that rats and moisture are a potent combination. Stocks depreciate, which means that the rate of return on storage is *negative* (a kilogram of maize stored today becomes less than a kilogram of maize tomorrow). An argument identical to the one we have just invoked for Becky's parents can now be used to show that Desta's parents would find it best to consume more in the weeks immediately following each harvest than in later weeks. This explains why Desta's family consume less and less and become physically weaker as the next harvest grows nearer. But Desta's parents have realized that the human body is a more productive bank

Corn dries in a storage enclosure in Botswana, preparatory to being ground into meal.

than the floor where they store their maize. So the family consumes even more maize than they otherwise would during the months following each harvest, but draw on the accumulated body mass during the weeks before the next harvest, by which time maize reserves will have been depleted. Across the years maize consumption assumes a sawtooth pattern, a practice that has been observed widely among households in subsistence agriculture. As Desta and her siblings contribute to daily household production, they are economically valuable assets. The transfer of resources in Desta's household, in contrast to Becky's, will be from the children to their parents.

Earlier we noted several reasons why people in sub-Saharan Africa aim to have large numbers of children. Desta has five siblings.

Unfortunately, high population growth has placed so much additional pressure on the local ecosystem, that the local commons that used to be managed reasonably well are now deteriorating. That they are is reflected in Desta's mother's complaint that the daily time and effort required to collect from the local commons has increased in recent years.

Firms

We define firms as institutions whose sole purpose is to produce goods and services for the market. Firms that move savings from those whose income and liquid assets exceeds their expenditure (young households, such as Becky's) and transfer them to those who wish to spend more than their income and liquid assets (retired people, such as Becky's grandparents) make up an economy's financial system. Financial institutions include banks, credit card companies, and savings and loan associations (in the UK they are known as "building societies"). Similarly, insurance firms enable people to transfer income across uncertain contingencies. Then there are firms that produce commodities (machine tools, repair services, food, and so on). Bankruptcy is a widespread phenomenon among firms. To give you a sense of the order of magnitude in Becky's world, although about 646,000 new businesses were incorporated in the US in 1990, about 642,000 businesses filed for bankruptcy that year. Evidently, firms appear and disappear.

Limited Liability and Joint Stock Companies

As with infrastructure (Chapter 4), manufacturing industries and even the retail sector enjoy economies of scale. In order to grow, a firm typically has to make large investments, meaning that it needs to spread its financial source of new investments widely. Proprietorships (single owners) and partnerships are unable to do that. A firm's owners are able to absorb greater risks if they acquire a charter that gives them the privilege of *limited liability*; which is when the firm is called a *corporation*. Corporations can raise capital by going "public" and issuing shares (known as the firm's stock). By purchasing a corporation's stock, an investor is entitled to a share of the firm's dividends. The corporation is liable for all its debts. In case it goes bankrupt, its assets are sold. The money obtained by selling its assets goes first to creditors (banks, bondholders); following which, if there is any money left, it goes to shareholders. If a corporation goes bankrupt, shareholders could well lose all the money they invested by purchasing its shares, but they won't lose any more than their original investment (that's limited liability).

That a firm has gone public means that its shares can be traded in the stock market. By allowing people to buy shares in diverse firms and to sell them when they wish to, the stock market enables investors to spread their risks even while saving for the future. The return from buying shares in a corporation is the dividend plus the capital gains (or losses) on the shares.

Corporations are able to finance new investments by (i) borrowing from the financial sector or by issuing bonds; (ii) retaining some of their earnings; or (iii) issuing more shares. From the point of view of shareholders, the ideal behavior on the part of a corporation's management would be one that maximizes the firm's stock market value. The problem is that no two shareholders are likely to agree what that ideal behavior is, nor is the management likely to agree with shareholders. Moreover, shareholders face a moral hazard because many of the management's activities are likely to be unverifiable. Share prices in

Wall Street stockbrokers are shown at work on the floor of the New York Stock Exchange in 2008.

the stock market aggregate the investors' beliefs about the risks involved in purchasing shares.

The ratio of a corporation debt to equity influences its management's incentives: too little debt, and management has little incentive to work hard for greater efficiency; too much debt, and the greater risk of bankruptcy disrupts the firm's behavior. A corporation's financial structure is therefore a signal to the outside world. It influences the market's beliefs about the firm's prospects. Seen from the point of view of management, issuing debt signals to stockholders that management have the incentives to work hard to protect and promote the firm's prospects. Moreover, in the US, interest payments on a firm's debt are tax deductible, but until recently dividends were not. These facts help to explain why established corporations finance most of their investments (in excess of retained earnings, that is) by borrowing from banks and issuing bonds. Today in the US more than 90% of new investment in corporations is financed by debt.

The emergence of the joint stock company with limited liability, which was consolidated in 1855 by the British Parliament's Limited Liability Act, is widely regarded to have been one of the most significant institutional innovations in business history. In the public's mind corporations reflect Big Business. That isn't entirely unjustified, but it misses much of the point. In the US, the number of corporations is less than 20% of the number of private firms, but they earn over 80% of the revenue. That said, the ability of households to spread their risks even while investing in far off places via the agency of corporate firms is an enormous advantage to society. It has been a significant factor behind the economic success of Becky's world.

SEVEN

Sustainable Economic Development

•

ECONOMIC GROWTH IS A GOOD THING. It may not buy happi-
ness (Chapter 2), but it usually purchases a better quality of life. Table
1 showed that growth in real GDP per capita comes hand in hand with
improvements in the way people are able to live. But can economies grow
indefinitely, or are there limits to growth? To put the question in a more
contemporary form, is growth in real GDP compatible with sustainable
economic development?

Conflicting Viewpoints

The question is several decades old. If discussions on it continue to be
shrill, it is because two opposing empirical perspectives have shaped them.

An aerial view illustrates suburban sprawl near Las Vegas, one of the nation's fastest-growing
metropolitan areas. The United States is the world's largest consumer of natural resources,
but many Americans are realizing that pursuit of prosperity—the American Dream—must be
tempered with conservation of resources.

On the one hand, if we look at specific examples of natural resources (fresh water, ocean fisheries, the atmosphere as a carbon sink—more generally, ecosystems), there is strong evidence that the rates at which we are currently utilizing them are unsustainable. During the twentieth century world population grew by a factor of four to more than 6 billion; industrial output increased by a multiple of 40 and the use of energy by 16; methane-producing cattle population grew in pace with human population; fish catch increased by a multiple of 35; and carbon and sulphur dioxide emissions by 10. The application of nitrogen to the terrestrial environment from the use of fertilizers, fossil fuels, and leguminous crops is now at least as great as that from all natural sources combined. Ecologists have estimated that 40% of the net energy created by terrestrial photosynthesis is currently being appropriated for human use. These figures put the scale of our presence on earth in perspective and reveal that Humanity has created an unprecedented disturbance in Nature in a brief period of a century or so.

On the other hand, it has been argued that just as earlier generations in Becky's world invested in science and technology, education, and machines and equipment so as to bequeath to her parents' generation the ability to achieve high income levels, they are now in turn making investments that will assure still higher living standards in the future. It has been argued as well that the historical trend in the prices of marketed natural resources, such as minerals and ores, has been so flat that there isn't any reason for alarm. Economic growth has allowed more people to have access to potable water and enjoy better protection against water- and air-borne diseases. The physical environment inside the home has improved beyond measure with economic growth: cooking in the Indian subcontinent continues to be a major cause of respiratory illnesses among women. Moreover, natural resources can be so shifted around today, that dwindling resources in one place can be met by imports from another. Intellectuals and commentators use the term "globalization" to imply that location *per se* doesn't matter. This optimistic view emphasizes the potential of capital accumulation and technological improvements to compensate for environmental degradation. It says that economic growth, even in the form and shape it has taken so far, *is* compatible with sustainable development. Which may explain why contemporary societies are obsessed with cultural survival and on the whole dismissive of any suggestion that we need to find ways to survive ecologically.

Strip mining, shown here in Colorado, is still common practice despite adverse environmental effects. In general, economists take into account mineral resources, fossil fuels, and arable land when estimating a nation's wealth in natural resources; however, fresh water, ocean fisheries, clean atmosphere, and healthy ecosystems are not factored into such metrics.

Broadly speaking, environmental scientists and activists hold the former view, while economists and economic commentators maintain the latter. It is no doubt banal to say that our economies are built in and on Nature, but I wonder if you noticed that the list of productive assets I drew earlier (Chapter 1) didn't include *natural capital*. Nature didn't feature in our account of macroeconomic history because it doesn't appear in official publications of the vital statistics of nations. The extraction of minerals and fossil fuels is included in modern national accounts (though not depreciated), but with the exception of agricultural land, natural capital makes very little appearance. If Nature's services have appeared in this book so far only in passing, it is because that is how matters are in the literature on the theory and empirics of economic growth and the economics of poverty.

Natural Capital: Classification

Natural capital is of direct use in consumption (fisheries); of indirect use as inputs in production (oil and natural gas); or of use in both (air and water). The value of a resource is often derived from its usefulness (as a source of food, or as an essential actor in ecosystems—such as a keystone species); but there are resources whose value is aesthetic (places of scenic beauty), or intrinsic (primates, blue whales, sacred groves), or a combination of all three (biodiversity). The worth of a natural resource could be based on what is extracted from it (timber), or on its presence as a stock (forest cover), or on both (watersheds).

The ecologists and environmental scientists Paul Ehrlich, John Holdren, Peter Raven, and more recently Gretchen Daily, Jane Lubchenco, Pamela Matson, Harold Mooney, and others have taught us the economic significance of ecosystems. Interpreting natural capital in an inclusive way, as I am doing here, allows us to add ecosystems to our list of capital assets.

The services they produce include maintaining a genetic library, preserving and regenerating soil, fixing nitrogen and carbon, recycling nutrients, controlling floods, filtering pollutants, assimilating waste, pollinating crops, operating the hydrological cycle, and maintaining the gaseous composition of the atmosphere. A number of them have a global reach (the atmosphere), but many are localized (microwatersheds).

Pollutants are the reverse of resources. Roughly speaking, "resources" are "goods" (in many situations they are the sinks into which pollutants are discharged), while "pollutants" (the degrader of resources) are "bads." If over a period of time the discharge of pollutants into a sink exceeds the latter's assimilative capacity, the sink collapses. Pollution is thus the reverse of conservation. In what follows, we will use the terms *natural resources* and *environment* interchangeably.

Two Simple Exercises in Environmental Economics

In order to demonstrate that economics is capable of joining the environmental sciences in a seamless way, it will prove useful to begin with a discussion of two issues that are much in the news today. The first is the subject of an acrimonious debate between those who favor free trade and those who are opposed to it on grounds that it often hurts the poorest in Desta's world. The second is the belief that because the economic effects of carbon dioxide emissions into the atmosphere are likely to be felt by a generation or two further down from us, we needn't do anything about climate change now.

Trade Expansion and the Environment

There should be little doubt today that, other things being equal, freeing trade enables economies to grow faster. A large body of empirical work testifies to that. There is some evidence too that the poor, *as a group*, also enjoy the fruits of faster growth. However, as the environmental consequences of economic growth are rarely assessed, the case for freeing trade remains unclear. If those consequences hurt many of the poorest in society, there is room for discussion about the merits of freeing trade without at the same time taking precautionary measures. Here is an example of how trade expansion can hurt.

An easy way for governments in poor countries that are richly covered in forests to earn revenue is to issue timber concessions to private logging firms. Imagine that logging concessions are awarded for the upland forest of a watershed. Deforestation contributes to an increase in siltation and the risk of floods downstream. If the law recognizes the rights of those who are harmed, the logging firm would have to compensate downstream farmers and coastal fishermen. But there is a gulf between the law and the enforcement of the law. When the cause of damage is miles away, when the timber concession has been awarded by the state, and when the victims are a scattered group of poor farmers and coastal fishermen, the issue of a negotiated outcome usually doesn't arise. It can even be that those who are harmed do not know the underlying cause of their deteriorating circumstances. If the logging firm isn't required to compensate those suffering damage, the private cost of logging is less than the true cost of logging, the latter being the sum of the costs borne by the logging firm and all who are adversely affected. From the country's point of view, timber exports are underpriced, which is another way of saying that there is excessive deforestation upstream. It is also a way of saying that there is an implicit subsidy on the export, paid for by people who are evicted from the forest and by people downstream. The subsidy is hidden from public scrutiny; but it amounts to a transfer of wealth from the exporting country to those that

A farmstead has been cleared in the Amazon rainforest in Peru, where farmers work the land claimed from the jungle. Although farmers benefit from this arable land, clear-cutting has many adverse environmental effects.

import the timber. Some of the poorest people in a poor country would be subsidizing the incomes of the average importer in a rich country.

Unfortunately, I can give you no idea of the magnitude of those subsidies, because they haven't been estimated. International organizations have the resources to undertake such studies; but, to the best of my knowledge, they haven't done so. The example shouldn't be used to argue against free trade, but it can be used to caution anyone who advocates free trade while ignoring its environmental impacts.

Discounting Climate Change

My second example concerns the emission of greenhouse gases and the global climate change it is inducing, the subject of continuing study by the Intergovernmental Panel on Climate Change (IPCC).

The global concentration of carbon dioxide in the atmosphere stood at approximately 260 parts per million (ppm) for 11,000 years until the early eighteenth century, but is now 380 ppm. (We will ignore the concentration of methane, which is another greenhouse gas.) The most reliable evidence on climate change over geological time comes from ice cores in Antarctica, which reveals that until the early eighteenth century, the maximum concentration of carbon dioxide during the previous 420,000 years was 300 ppm. That long interval of time witnessed four glacial-interglacial cycles, each of about 100,000 years' duration. Those cycles are driven by rhythmic changes in the amount of solar radiation reaching Earth, the effects of which are amplified by the feedbacks and forces they in turn generate within Earth's environment.

We are living in an interglacial period, which means that Earth is experiencing a warm phase. If current trends in carbon emissions continue, carbon concentration is expected to reach 500 ppm (which is nearly twice the pre-industrial level) by the middle of this century, and could reach as high a figure as 750 ppm (which is nearly three times the pre-industrial level) by the year 2100. A doubling of present-day carbon concentration is expected to give rise to an increase in the mean global atmospheric temperature by 3 to 7 degrees Celsius. With a trebling of concentration, it could rise by 6 to 11 degrees. The temperature that would result even if the rise were limited to 3 degrees is beyond anything that has been experienced on Earth in the past 420,000 years. The *speed* of that change is of particular significance, because it would mean that a good portion of our capital assets will become less than useful long before their planned obsolescence. Some of our infrastructure will even disappear under the rising seas. In order to restructure our assets, humanity will need to make additional investments, diverting resources from consumption. If we add the impact of rapid climate change on ecosystems (changes in the disease environment to which human populations are not immune; degradation in the composition, geographic distribution, and productivity of ecosystems), the potential costs begin to look huge. Nevertheless, when in 2004 eight eminent economists were invited to Copenhagen to offer advice on how the world community could most usefully spend $50 billion over a five-year period, they placed climate change at the bottom of their list of ten alternatives.

Why did the economists do that? They did it because their reasoning was based on discounting future costs and benefits at a positive rate. Reducing global carbon emissions or investing in technologies for carbon sequestration would involve huge costs now, but the benefits from averting economic disruptions would be enjoyed only 50 to 100 years from now. Long-term interest rates on government bonds in the US have been 3–5% a year. When economists there evaluate *public* projects, they typically use such a figure to discount future benefits and costs, regarding it as the "opportunity cost of capital," the term being applied to the rate of interest that could be earned by investing in government bonds rather than in the project whose benefits and costs are being evaluated. At discount rates of 3–5%, though, consumption benefits in the distant future look minute today. If you discount at 4% a year, a dollar's worth of additional consumption benefits 100 years from now would be worth less than 3 cents today; which is another way of saying that as a price for giving up $1 worth of consumption today, you would demand that more than $30 worth of consumption benefits be made available 100 years from now. A number of economic models of climate change have shown that if you use an annual discount rate of, say, 4%, the costs (which are negative benefits) are greater than the sum of the discounted benefits from curbing net carbon emissions. Doing something about climate change now, the calculations imply, would be to throw money away on a comparatively bad project.

Should the global community discount future consumption benefits at a positive rate? As with households at the private level (Chapter 6), so it is with households at the collective level: there are two reasons why it may be reasonable for the global community to discount future benefits at a positive rate. First, a future benefit would be of less value than that same benefit today if the global community is impatient to enjoy the benefit now. Impatience is a reason for discounting future costs and benefits at a positive rate. Second, considerations of justice and equality demand that consumption per capita should be smoothed across the generations. So, if future generations are likely to be richer than us, there is a case for valuing an extra dollar's worth of their consumption less than an extra dollar's worth of our consumption, other things being equal. Rising consumption per capita provides a second justification for discounting future costs and benefits at a positive rate.

Philosophers have argued that societal impatience is ethically indefensible, because it favors policies that discriminate against future generations merely on the grounds that they are not present today. Once we accept their argument, we are left with only the second reason for discounting future costs and benefits. But if rising per capita consumption provides the global community with a reason for discounting future consumption benefits at a positive rate, declining per capita consumption would provide it with a reason for discounting future consumption benefits at a *negative* rate. We noted the latter possibility at the household level in connection with the dilemma Desta's parents face when deciding how to spread the consumption of maize between harvests (Chapter 6).

Economists use positive discount rates in their models of climate change because the models *assume* that global consumption per head will continue to grow over the next 150 years and more even if net emissions of greenhouse gases follow current trends; which is to assume that climate change poses no serious threat to the future. But an increase in the mean global temperature by 3–5 degrees Celsius would take the biosphere into a climatic zone that has not been visited in *millions* of years on Earth. The possible consequences of such changes to our productive base are so huge, that it isn't to be an alarmist to question forecasts of continual economic growth even after Earth enters that zone. Suppose you fear that if nothing substantial is done today to discover ways to sequester carbon and to find alternatives to fossil fuels as sources of energy, there is a sizeable chance that global consumption per head, suitably weighted across regions and income groups, will decline—owing, say, to a big increase in the frequency of extreme weather events, more severe droughts in the tropics, the emergence of new pathogens, and degradation of vital ecosystems. You should then use a negative rate to discount future consumption benefits. Notice though that applying a negative rate *amplifies* benefits in the distant future when viewed from the present, it doesn't attenuate them.

Let us perform a quick calculation to get a feel for orders of magnitude. Empirical evidence from societal and personal choices suggests that the rate a society ought to use to discount future consumption benefits is about three times the percentage rate of change of consumption per capita. Imagine that carbon emissions follow their current trends (which is often called "business as usual"). Consider a scenario in which global consumption per capita increases at an annual rate of 0.5% for the next 50 years and declines at 1% a year for the following 100 years. Under that scenario, the global community ought to discount future consumption benefits at 1.5% a year for the next 50 years (3 times 0.5) and at *minus* 3% for the subsequent 100 years (3 times minus 1). A simple calculation now shows that a dollar's worth of additional consumption 150 years from now is worth $9 of additional consumption today. To put it another way, the global community should be willing to forgo $9 worth of additional consumption today for an extra dollar's worth of consumption benefits 150 years in the future. The calculation reverses the message that has been conveyed by economic models of climate change.

There should be little doubt that private investors would be using a positive rate to discount their personal earnings even under the above scenario. They would be doing so because the interest rate offered by commercial banks on deposits would most likely remain positive. But there is no contradiction here. Under "business as usual," the atmosphere is an open access resource. So long as people are free to emit carbon dioxide, there will be a wedge between private rates of return on investment and the rates the world community ought to use to discount collective costs and benefits. The former could be positive even while the latter is negative. That wedge is a reason for controlling carbon emissions into the atmosphere and bringing the two rates closer to each other; it isn't a reason for claiming that the problem of global climate change should be shelved for the future.

The effects of rising global temperatures are evidenced by glacial retreat and shrinking ice caps across the world. This NASA image shows Himalayan lakes formed by glaciers that have been melting during recent decades.

GDP and the Productive Base

What we have just conducted are but a pair of finger exercises. Nevertheless, they have shown us how natural capital can be introduced in microeconomic reasoning. Let us see if it can be included in macroeconomic reasoning.

A famous 1987 report by an international commission (widely known as the Brundtland Commission Report) defined *sustainable development* as ". . . development that meets the needs of the present without compromising the ability of future generations to meet their own needs." In this reckoning, sustainable development requires that relative to their populations each generation should bequeath to its successor at least as large a *productive base* as it had itself inherited. Notice that the requirement is derived from a relatively weak notion of intergenerational justice. Sustainable development demands that future generations have no less of the means to meet their needs than we do ourselves; it demands nothing more. But how is a generation to judge whether it is leaving behind an adequate productive base for its successor?

It is easy to see why focusing on GDP won't do. An economy's productive base is its stock of capital assets and institutions (Chapter 1). By capital assets, we now mean not only manufactured capital, human capital, and knowledge—which is what we limited ourselves to in Chapter 1—but also natural capital. We will presently discover what to look for in order to check whether an economy's productive base is expanding or contracting. It is evident, though, that an economy's productive base will shrink if its stock of capital assets depreciates and its institutions aren't able to improve sufficiently to compensate for that depreciation. GDP is an acronym for *gross* domestic product. The word *gross* means that GDP ignores the depreciation of capital assets. It is certainly possible for a country's productive base to grow while its GDP increases (this will be confirmed when we come to study Table 2 on page 170), which is no doubt a path of economic development we all would like to follow; but it is also possible for a country's productive base to *shrink* during a period when GDP grows (this also will be confirmed when we come to study Table 2). The problem is that no one would notice the shrinking if everyone's eyes were riveted on GDP. If the productive base continues to shrink, economic growth will sooner or later stop and reverse sign. The standard of living will then decline, but no one would have suspected that a fall was in store. So, growth in GDP per head can encourage us to think that all is well, when it isn't. Similarly, it is possible for a country's Human Development Index (HDI; Chapter 1) to increase even while its productive base shrinks (Table 2). This means that HDI too can mislead.

Market Prices as Signals of Resource Scarcity

You could counter that a fixation on GDP or HDI shouldn't prevent anyone from looking up prices. You could even argue that if natural resources really were becoming more scarce, their prices would have risen, and that would have signaled that all is not well. But if prices are to reveal scarcities, markets must function well (Chapter 4). For many natural resources, markets not only don't function well, they don't even exist (we called them "missing markets" earlier). In some cases, they don't exist because relevant economic interactions take place over large distances, making the costs of negotiation too high (for example, the effects of upland deforestation on downstream farming and fishing activities); in other cases, they don't exist because the interactions are separated by large temporal distances (for example, the effect of carbon emission on climate in the distant future, in a world where forward markets don't exist because future generations are not present today to negotiate with us). Then there are cases (the atmosphere, aquifers, the open seas) where the migratory nature of the resource keeps markets from existing—they are open access resources (Chapter 2); while in others, ill-specified or unprotected property rights prevent markets from being formed (mangroves and coral reefs), or make them function wrongly even when they do form (those who are displaced by deforestation aren't compensated). Earlier, we called the side effects of human activities that are undertaken without mutual agreement, "externalities."

Our dealings with Nature are full of externalities. The examples suggest that the externalities involving the environment are mostly negative, implying that the private costs of using natural resources are less than their social costs. Being underpriced, the environment is over-exploited. In such a situation, the economy could enjoy growth in real GDP and improvements in HDI for a long spell even while its productive base shrinks. As proposals for estimating the social scarcity prices of natural resources remain contentious, economic accountants ignore them and governments remain wary of taxing their use.

The Environment: Is It a Luxury or Necessity?

It isn't uncommon to regard the environment as a luxury good, as in the thought expressed in a prominent newspaper that "economic growth is good for the environment because countries need to put poverty behind them in order to care." But in Desta's world the environment is an essential factor of production. When wetlands, inland and coastal fisheries, woodlands, forests, ponds, and grazing fields are damaged (owing to agricultural encroachment, nitrogen overload, urban extensions, the construction of large dams, resource usurpation by the state, or whatever), it is the rural poor who suffer most. Frequently, there are no alternative sources of livelihood for them. In contrast, for rich eco-tourists or importers of primary products, there is something else, often somewhere else; which means that there are alternatives. Degradation of ecosystems is like the depreciation of roads, buildings, and machinery—but with two big differences: (i) it is frequently irreversible (or at best the system takes a long time to recover), and (ii) ecosystems can collapse abruptly, without much prior warning. Imagine what would happen to a city's inhabitants if the infrastructure connecting it

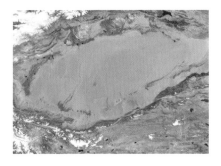

Climate change has led to rapid desertification in many regions of the world, in some cases with sand dunes encroaching upon vegetation. Sand dunes in northwest China's Taklimakan Desert, seen in this satellite image, are shifting into the pastures and fields of herders and farmers at the desert's edge.

to the outside world was to break down without notice. Vanishing water holes, deteriorating grazing fields, barren slopes, and wasting mangroves are spatially confined instances of corresponding breakdowns among the rural poor in Desta's world. The analysis in Chapter 2 can now be invoked to explain how an abrupt ecological collapse—such as the one that has been experienced in recent years in the Horn of Africa and the Darfur region of Sudan—can trigger a rapid socio-economic decline.

Sustainable Development: Theory and Evidence

Economic development is sustainable if, relative to its population, a society's productive base doesn't shrink. How can one tell whether economic development has been sustainable? We have noted that neither GDP nor HDI will tell us. So what index would do the job? A society's productive base is its institutions and capital assets. As we are interested in estimating the change in an economy's productive base over a period of time, we need to know how to combine the changes that take place in its capital stocks and in its institutions. Let us keep institutions aside for the moment and concentrate on capital assets.

Intuitively, it is clear that we have to do more than just keep a score of capital assets (so many additional pieces of machinery and equipment;

so many more miles of roads; so many fewer square miles of forest cover; and so forth). An economy's productive base declines if the decumulation of assets is not compensated by the accumulation of other assets. Contrarywise, the productive base expands if the decumulation of assets *is* (more than) compensated by the accumulation of other assets. The ability of an asset to compensate for the decline in some other asset depends on technological knowledge (for example, double glazing can substitute for central heating up to a point, but only up to a point) and on the quantities of assets the economy happens to have in stock (for example, the protection trees provide against soil erosion depends on the existing grass cover). Clearly, though, capital assets differ in their ability to compensate for one another. Those abilities are the *values* we would wish to impute to assets. We need to have estimates of those abilities. This is where an asset's *social productivity* becomes an item of interest. By an asset's social productivity, we mean the net increase in *social well-being* that would be enjoyed if an additional unit of that asset were made available to the economy, other things being equal. Putting it another way, the social productivity of an asset is the capitalized value of the flow of services an extra unit of it would provide society. An asset's value is simply its quantity multiplied by its social productivity.

As we are trying to make operational sense of the concept of *sustainable* development, we must include in the term "social well-being" not only the well-being of those who are present, but also of those who will be here in the future. There are ethical theories that go beyond a purely anthropocentric view of Nature, by insisting that certain aspects of Nature have intrinsic value. The concept of social well-being I am appealing to here includes intrinsic values in its net if required. However, an ethical theory on its own won't be enough to determine the social productivities of capital assets, because there would be nothing for the theory to act upon. We need *descriptions* of states of affairs too. To add a unit of a capital asset to an economy is to perturb that economy. In order to estimate the contribution of that additional unit to social well-being, we need a description of the state of affairs both before and after the addition has been made. In short, measuring the social productivities of capital assets involves both evaluation and description.

Imagine now that you have adopted a conception of social well-being (by adding the well-beings of all persons) and that you have an economic scenario of the future in mind (business as usual). In principle you can now estimate the social productivity of every capital asset. You can do that by estimating the contribution to social well-being (that's the evaluative part of the exercise) an additional unit of each capital asset would make, *other things being equal* (that's the descriptive part of the exercise). Economists call social productivities of capital assets their *shadow prices*, to distinguish them from prices that are observed in the market. Although shadow prices pertain to commodities generally, not only to capital assets, we focus on capital assets here.

Shadow prices reflect the social scarcities of capital assets. In the world as we know it, estimating shadow prices is a formidable problem. There are ethical values we hold that are probably impossible to commensurate when they come up against other values that we also hold. This doesn't mean ethical values don't impose bounds on shadow prices; they do. Which is why the language of shadow prices is essential if we wish to avoid making somber pronouncements about sustainable development that amount to saying nothing. Most methods that are currently deployed to estimate the shadow prices of ecosystem services are crude, but deploying them is a lot better than doing nothing to value them.

The value of an economy's stock of capital assets, measured in terms of their shadow prices, is its *inclusive wealth*. The term *inclusive* serves to remind us not only that natural capital has been included on the list of assets, but also that externalities have been taken into account in valuing the assets. Inclusive wealth is the sum of the values of all capital assets. It is a number—expressed, say, in international dollars.

We can summarize by saying that an economy's inclusive wealth plus institutions constitute its productive base. If we now wish to determine whether a country's economic development has been sustainable over a period of time, we have to estimate the changes that took place over that period in its inclusive wealth and its institutions—relative to population of course. In Chapter 1 we noted that changes in knowledge and institutions over time are reflected in changes in total factor productivity. So we break up the procedure for estimating changes in an economy's productive base relative to population during any period of time into five stages.

First, estimate the value of changes in the amounts and compositions of manufactured capital, human capital, and natural capital—which we will call *inclusive investment*. (If inclusive investment is found to be positive, we may conclude that manufactured capital, human capital, and natural capital, taken together, grew over the period.) Second, estimate the change in total factor productivity. Third, transform the two figures in a way that enables us to calculate the effects of the two sets of changes on the productive base. Fourth, combine the two resulting estimates into a single number that can be taken to reflect the change that took place in the economy's productive base. Fifth, make a correction for demographic changes to arrive at an estimate for the change that took place in the economy's productive base relative to population.

I have so worded the five steps that they apply to a study of the past. But, of course, the five steps can be applied with equal validity to forecasts of the future. The procedure outlined here is essential for anyone who wants to know whether the economic pathways we are currently pursuing can be expected to lead to sustainable development.

Has Economic Development in Recent Decades Been Sustainable?

Recently, economists at the World Bank have estimated inclusive investment in different countries during the past few decades. They have done that by adding net investment in human capital to existing country-wide estimates of investment in manufactured capital, and then subtracting *dis*investments in natural capital from that sum. (That's step 1 on page 166.) The economists used official estimates of net national saving as proxies for net investment in manufactured capital. For estimates of investment in human capital, they used expenditure on education as a proxy. To quantify disinvestments in natural capital, they considered net changes in the stocks of commercial forests, oil and minerals, and the quality of the atmosphere in terms of its carbon dioxide content. Oil and minerals were valued at their market prices minus extraction costs. The shadow price of global carbon emission into the atmosphere is the damage caused by bringing about climate change. That damage was taken to be $20 per ton, which is in all probability a serious underestimate. Forests were valued in terms of their market price minus logging costs. Contributions of forests to ecosystem functions were ignored.

The World Bank's list of natural resources is incomplete. It doesn't include water resources, fisheries, air and water pollutants, soil, and ecosystems. Their notion of human capital is inadequate because health does not

World Bank and International Monetary Fund delegates attend the seventy-ninth meeting of the Development Committee at the World Bank headquarters in Washington, D.C., in 2009. The stated goal of the committee is to assist the economies of developing nations.

enter the calculus. And their estimates of shadow prices are very approximate. Nevertheless, one has to start somewhere, and theirs is a first pass at what is an enormously messy enterprise. What I want to do now is to study figures published recently by a group of ecologists and economists, who adapted the World Bank estimates of inclusive investment and then went on to determine whether economic development in some of the major countries and regions in Desta's and Becky's worlds has been sustainable in recent decades. Table 2 on page 170 is a refinement of that publication. It remains a crude beginning to the study of sustainable development, but it's a start.

The places in question are sub-Saharan Africa, Bangladesh, India, Nepal, and Pakistan (all poor countries); China (a middle-income country); and the UK and US (both rich countries). The period under study is 1970–2000. The first column of numbers in Table 2 consists of refinements of the World Bank's estimates of average inclusive investment as a proportion of GDP, expressed as percentages (step 1). The second column gives the average annual population growth rate. The third column gives estimates of annual growth rates of total factor productivity, which we are interpreting here as the annual percentage rate of change in a combined index of knowledge and institutions (that's step 2). I have used the figures in the first three columns to arrive at estimates of the annual percentage rate of change in the productive base per capita (that involves a combination of steps 3–5). They are given in the fourth column.

Before summarizing the findings, it will be useful to get a feel for what the numbers in the table are telling us. Consider Pakistan. During 1970–2000 inclusive, investment as a proportion of GDP was 8.8% annually. Total factor productivity increased at an annual rate of 0.4%. As both figures are positive, we can conclude that Pakistan's productive base was larger in 2000 than it had been in 1970. But take a look at Pakistan's population, which grew at a high 2.7% rate annually. The fourth column shows that Pakistan's productive base per capita declined in consequence, at an annual rate of 0.7%, implying that in 2000 it was about 80% of what it was in 1970.

In contrast, consider the US Inclusive investment as a share of GDP there was 8.9% a year, which is only a tiny bit larger than Pakistan's figure. Growth in total factor productivity (an annual 0.2%) was even lower than Pakistan's. But population grew only at 1.1% a year, meaning that the productive base per capita of the US grew at an average annual rate of 1%. Economic development in the US was sustainable during 1970–2000, while in Pakistan it was unsustainable.

Country/Region	I/Y* (percentage)	% Annual growth rate 1970–2000				
		Population (per head)	TFP†	Productive base (per head)	GDP (per head)	ΔHD/††
Sub-Saharan Africa	−2.1	2.7	0.1	−2.9	−0.1	+
Bangladesh	7.1	2.2	0.7	0.1	1.9	+
India	9.5	2.0	0.6	0.4	3.0	+
Nepal	13.3	2.2	0.5	0.6	1.9	+
Pakistan	8.8	2.7	0.4	−0.7	2.2	+
China	22.7	1.4	3.6	7.8	7.8	+
United Kingdom	7.4	0.2	0.7	2.4	2.2	+
US	8.9	1.1	0.2	1.0	1.1	+

*inclusive investment as a share of GDP (average over 1970–2000)
† total factor productivity
†† change in HDI between 1970 and 2000

Adapted from K. J. Arrow, P. Dasgupta, L. Goulder, G. Daily, P. R. Ehrlich, G. M. Heal, S. Levin, K.-G. Maler, S. Schneider, D. A. Starrett, and B. Walker, "Are We Consuming Too Much?," *Journal of Economic Perspectives*, 2004, Vol. 18, No. 3, pp. 147–172.

Table 2. The progress of nations

Interestingly, if you had judged their economic performances in terms of growth in GDP per capita, you would have obtained a different picture. As the fifth column of Table 2 shows, Pakistan grew at a respectable 2.2% rate a year, while the US grew at only 1.1% a year. If you now look at the sixth column, you will find that the United Nations' Human Development Index (HDI) for Pakistan improved during the period. Movements in HDI tell us nothing about sustainable development.

The striking message of Table 2, however, is that during 1970–2000 economic development in *all* the poor countries on our list was either unsustainable or barely sustainable. To be sure, sub-Saharan Africa offers no surprise. Its inclusive investment was *negative*, implying that the region *dis*invested in manufactured, human, and natural capital, taken together, at 2.1% of GDP. Population grew at 2.7% a year and total factor productivity barely advanced (annual growth rate: 0.1%). Even without performing any calculation, we should suspect that the productive base per capita in sub-Saharan Africa declined. The table confirms that it did, at 2.9% annually. If you now look at the fifth column of numbers, you will discover that GDP per capita in sub-Saharan Africa remained pretty much constant. But the region's HDI showed an improvement—confirming once again that studying movements in HDI enables us to say nothing about sustainable development.

Pakistan is the worst performer in the Indian subcontinent, but the remaining countries in the region just barely made it when judged in terms of sustainable development. Inclusive investment in each country (Bangladesh, India, and Nepal) was positive, as was growth in total factor productivity. The two together imply that the productive base expanded in each country. But population growth was so high, that the productive base per capita just about grew—at annual percentage rates 0.1, 0.4, and

0.6 respectively. Even these figures are most likely to be overestimates. The list of items the World Bank's economists used in order to estimate inclusive investment didn't include soil erosion and urban pollution, both of which are thought by experts to be problematic in the Indian subcontinent. Moreover, the human desire to reduce risk, mentioned earlier, implies that downside risks of natural capital degradation ought to be given a higher weight than a corresponding chance that things will turn out to be better than expected. So, if we allow for risk aversion, estimates of inclusive investment would be lowered. One cannot help suspecting that economic development in the Indian subcontinent was unsustainable during 1970–2000. But you wouldn't know that from figures for GDP per capita and HDI there. The former grew in each country in the region and the latter improved.

Inclusive investment in China was 22.7% of GDP, a very large figure in the sample of countries in Table 2. Growth in total factor productivity

was a high 3.6% annually. Population grew at a relatively low 1.4% annual rate. We shouldn't be surprised that China's productive base per capita expanded—as it happens, at 7.8% annually. Per capita GDP also grew at an annual rate of 7.8%, and HDI improved. In China, GDP per capita, HDI, and the productive base per head moved parallel to one another.

The state-owned Oil & Gas Development Corporation headquarters in Islamabad, Pakistan, dominates the surrounding landscape. Despite modernization and a burgeoning industrial sector, Pakistan's economic well-being is hampered by rapid population growth.

There is little to comment on the UK and US. Both are rich, mature economies. Inclusive investment during 1970–2000 was modest, but then so was population growth low. Growth in total factor productivity was low. Although the figures imply that the productive base per capita expanded in both countries, we should be circumspect because, as noted earlier, the World Bank costed carbon emissions at too low a rate. GDP per capita increased in both countries and HDI improved there.

The figures we have just studied are all rough and ready, but they show how accounting for natural capital can make a substantial difference to our conception of the development process. In Table 2, I have deliberately made conservative assumptions about the degradation of natural capital. For example, a price of $20 per ton of carbon in the atmosphere is almost certainly below its true social cost (or negative shadow price). If we were instead to take the shadow price to be the not unreasonable figure of $75 per ton, all the poor countries in Table 2 would show a decline in their productive base per capita during 1970–2000. The message we should take away is sobering: over the past three decades, sub-Saharan Africa (home to 750 million people today) has become poorer if judged in terms of its productive base per capita; and economic development in the Indian subcontinent (home to over 1.4 billion people today) was either unsustainable or just barely sustainable. That said, it would be wrong to conclude that people in poor countries should have invested more in their productive base by consuming less. We have noted repeatedly in this book that in Desta's world the production and distribution of goods and services are highly inefficient. It would be wrong to regard consumption and investment in the productive base there as competing for a fixed quantity of funds. Better institutions would enable people in Desta's world to both consume more and invest more (inclusively, of course!).

EIGHT

Social Well-being and Democratic Government

•

DURING THE 1970S, THE ECONOMIST Peter Bauer frequently wrote that if governments in today's poor countries had been diligent at what they are supposed to do—protect citizens from external threat by diplomacy, enforce the rule of law, provide public infrastructure (durable roads; ports; reliable administration; access to potable water and power), and enable markets to operate unhindered—they would have had no time nor resources left to mishandle their economies by interfering with trade, subsidizing favored industries, procuring agricultural products from farmers at administered prices, and installing public industries that turned into white elephants. Bauer's was something of a lone voice among development economists; and although his list of government responsibilities was incomplete,

Iranian supporters of candidate Mir-Hossein Moussavi fill the streets of Tehran to protest the results of the 2009 presidential election—an election that also brought condemnation from the international community. In an interconnected global economy, political turmoil and authoritarianism can result in debilitating economic sanctions.

by drawing attention to them he showed other development experts that economics has much to say about governance.

There are many pathways by which societies can muff their chances, but only a few by which they are able to prosper. In this monograph we began by identifying the contexts in which people who have agreed to do something can trust one another to keep their word. We then studied two micro institutions—households and firms—and two wide-ranging institutions within which households and firms are able to interact among one another, namely, communities and markets. We have now come close to getting a sense of the type of interplay among institutions and public policies that best enables people to flourish. In this chapter we will study the desirable motivation, reach and scope of an institution that in its ideal form supplements other institutions and arches over them in order that they are able to function well. That institution is *government*.

Freedom and Democracy

The government is an agency of its nation's citizens. It is answerable to them. (In contemporary democracies the term "civil *servant*" is applied to some of the most powerful people in the country.) Today we take those strictures to be self-evident, but it wasn't always so taken. In his 1949 (Alfred) Marshall Lectures at the University of Cambridge, the sociologist T. H. Marshall codified the modern concept of citizenship by identifying three social revolutions that took place in Europe: that of civil liberties in the eighteenth century, political liberties in the nineteenth, and socio-economic liberties in the twentieth. Marshall's historical account could suggest that "freedom" is a fetish peculiar to Becky's world, but that would be a mistake. I don't know of any evidence that people in Desta's world don't wish to choose their political leaders or that they appreciate being ordered to move on by the authorities when congregating to discuss life in general and the quality of public services in particular. It is true that intellectuals ask whether poor countries can *afford* political and civil liberties—in common parlance the term *democracy* is frequently taken to subsume both—but that question has to do with the possibility that democracy hinders economic growth (worse, that it encourages unsustainable economic development), something citizens in poor countries would be expected to care about and would be justified in doing so.

The political scientist Seymour Martin Lipset famously observed that economic growth promotes democratic practice. The converse, that democracy promotes material prosperity, has been suggested by a number of social thinkers. So democracy has been seen not only as an end in itself, some have seen it also as a means to economic progress. Given their predilection for autocratic behavior, rulers in Desta's part of the world have thought otherwise. That democracy and economic growth involve trade-offs when countries are poor has been the stated belief of those in power in many of today's poorest countries.

Authoritarianism is superficially attractive because it's capable of offering firm governance. That a government should be firm isn't to be doubted; the difficult question is what the government should be firm *about*. The rule of law is a prime candidate. Among other things, it enables citizens to pursue their projects and purposes. Unhappily, in Desta's world authoritarian regimes have routinely violated that most fundamental of state obligations: respect for the rule of law. Earlier we noted that social norms of behavior holding communities together can collapse if the government is bent on destroying them. Rulers have long known that terrorism is a means by which they could impoverish relationships within communities so as to prevent any challenge to their rule.

In many instances autocracies in Desta's world have maintained their power by instilling fear among citizens. In more benign political climates, cronyism among public officials and government theft have kept citizens impoverished and those in authority in splendor.

But authoritarianism comes in all shapes and sizes. There are authoritarian regimes in the contemporary world that have enforced the rule of law and enabled citizens to prosper materially (Singapore is an example). They have been known to install checks and balances in public administration and correct policy errors. But they are exceptions. And the problem with exceptions is that they don't offer much guidance to others. After all, citizens can't be expected to will wise authoritarianism into existence, nor can they easily remove an authoritarian regime if the political leadership proves to be unsound or rapacious. On the other hand, democracy can't guarantee economic progress either. What democracy can do is to give citizens the chance to coordinate among themselves—say, by civic engagement (Chapters 2–3)—in order to make the state enforce the rule of law and provide those other essential public services that enable people to try to make something of their lives. But political pluralism can coexist with civic irresponsibility even to an extent that no one has an incentive to do anything about the latter. In the language of Chapter 2, democracy allied to a chaotic social order is an equilibrium, just as democracy allied to a social order where citizens are decent to one another is an equilibrium. We have approximations to both in the contemporary world.

Statistical analysis of data covering the past four decades suggests that, among poor countries, those where citizens had enjoyed greater democracy had, on average, also enjoyed higher economic growth. Correlation isn't causation, but the finding hints at the possibility that democracy isn't a luxury in poor countries. That said, there have been few such empirical studies, so we don't know whether the finding is empirically robust. More importantly, no one so far has investigated whether there is a positive link between democracy and growth in the productive base per capita; which means that, as matters stand, we don't know the connection between democracy and sustainable development in the contemporary world. Democracy means many things at once—regular and fair elections, government transparency, political pluralism, a free press, freedom of association, freedom to complain about degradation of the natural environment, and so on. We still have little empirical understanding of which aspects are most instrumental in bringing about sustainable development. That being so, a commitment to democracy today can't be based on grounds that it promotes sustainable development. We should favor democracy because (i) it is innately a good thing and (ii) it isn't known to hinder economic progress and may possibly even help to bring it about.

Well-being: Individual and Social

What kinds of social institutions and what types of public policies are most likely to enable people to flourish? At the core of that question is the notion of a person's *well-being*, by which we mean, broadly speaking, the degree to which the person is able to exercise independence, choice, and self-determination. The centrality of social institutions in the realization of well-being is clear enough: social life is an expression of a person's sense of social unity, and commodities and an absence of coercion are the means by which people can pursue their own conception of the good. T. H. Marshall's three-way classification of freedom can be read as saying that the enjoyment of civil liberties, the ability to participate in the political sphere, and access to commodities (food, clothing, shelter, health care, education—more generally, wealth) are necessary if people are to flourish.

Constituents and Determinants

Marshall's classification can be broken up into smaller components. Various kinds of civil liberty, various aspects of health, and so on, comprise the *constituents* of well-being. As well-being itself is an aggregate, measuring someone's well-being involves an aggregation exercise, which means acknowledging trade-offs among the constituents.

We have seen that there is another way to think about human well-being. It involves valuing well-being's *determinants*, by which I mean the commodity inputs that produce well-being. The determinants include not only such necessities as food and shelter, but also access to knowledge and information. One may think of the constituents and determinants of well-being as "ends" and "means," respectively. In practical applications it proves useful to aggregate the determinants of well-being into a single figure. In the previous chapter I argued that a person's inclusive wealth can be made to serve as an aggregate index of her well-being.

Revealed and Stated Preferences

How is one to assess someone's well-being? There are aspects that can be inferred from the choices people make. If someone is found to purchase and read an unusual number of books, it may be reasonable to assume that her well-being depends, among other things, on whether she has books to read. This kind of assessment is known as the method of *revealed preference*. The underlying logic here is that, other things being equal, a person reveals her wants and desires by the choices she makes, whether in markets or in communities.

There are, however, aspects of well-being that can only be ascertained by asking people to *state* them. They involve cases where the determinants are goods and services on which people are unable to express their preferences and interests because there is no opportunity for them to do so. Public goods and ecological services are examples. Care has to be taken to design questions in such ways as to minimize the risk that people don't respond truthfully. In recent years cunning methods have been devised by economists to ensure that people don't exaggerate their fondness for those goods, especially in circumstances where they don't have to pay for them.

Merit Goods

There are aspects of well-being that can be measured objectively. The medical, nutrition, and education needs of people are routinely assessed by experts. We may express doubt that experts know what they are talking about, but deep down we know that they know more about certain aspects of ourselves than we do. The economist Richard Musgrave argued many years ago that inferring well-being exclusively from revealed preference is wrong because of the presence of what he called *merit goods*. Merit goods protect and promote human interests, they don't merely serve our preferences. Merit goods are therefore worth more than what would be revealed from the choices people make. Philosophers have argued, for example, that we shouldn't seek to justify democracy exclusively from the intensity of the desires citizens display for democracy. Democracy is a merit good. Human rights also constitute a class of merit goods, among which "fundamental" rights are an extreme form, in that they aren't tradable. Rights don't go against preferences, of course; what they do is to reinforce some preferences (such as the preference not to be coerced) against the claims of other, less urgent or vital, preferences and interests.

It isn't always possible to discover the merits of goods from stated preferences either. The problem in part lies in the possibility that individuals don't tell the truth when asked, but in part it lies elsewhere. It would be an odd thing, for example, to say that there is little need to invest in women's reproductive health programs in Desta's world

Kenyan children orphaned by AIDS attend school in 2004. Health and education programs are merit goods, which protect and promote human interests.

because poor women there are resigned to their fate and don't appear much to insist on them; or that governments there ought not to invest in primary education because parents there don't care for education, and the children, being unaware of education, don't care either. Nor have I ever heard anyone so argue.

That said, it is salutary to be cautious when attributing "merit" to goods. An enthusiasm for seeing merit in goods can be a code for paternalism, even authoritarianism. The notion of "false consciousness" has been used by both secular and religious tyrannies in Desta's world to justify their actions ("My people don't know what is in their real interest," or "My followers depend on me to explain the Holy Book to them"). In an opposite vein, rights have proliferated in Becky's world to an extent that the very notion of rights is now debased. It is one thing to insist on the right not to be imprisoned indefinitely without being charged, it is quite another thing to claim that a 35-hour work week is a human right. The latter is an agreement won over the bargaining table, allied to some agitation; but it is a misuse of the term to call the outcomes of such agreements "rights" without further qualification.

Aggregation across People and Policy Evaluation

Social well-being is an aggregate of individual well-beings. Economists have, generally speaking, aggregated individual well-beings by summing them. In the previous chapter I had adopted that viewpoint by regarding social well-being as the sum of the current generation's and all future generations' well-beings, although nothing conceptual depended on that mode of aggregation. We noted there that movements in inclusive wealth over time measure changes in intergenerational well-being over time in terms of the commodity determinants of well-being. Those determinants are valued in terms of their shadow prices. It can be shown that in order to evaluate *policy* (for example, a new public investment; a change in the structure of taxes), the government should value alterations to the mix of goods and services brought about by the policy in terms of shadow prices. Such an evaluative exercise is called *social cost-benefit analysis*. The idea is to estimate the (social) profitability of the policy in terms of shadow prices and to recommend the policy if (and only if) the net social profit is positive. Thus, shadow prices are of use both in assessing sustainable development (Chapter 7) and in evaluating policies. This is one of those beautiful facts that economists are fortunate to unearth from time to time.

Functions of Government

The government is a major actor in every economy today. Its expenditure as a share of GDP is 18% in Desta's world and 28% in Becky's world. (The corresponding share in the European Union is 37%.) The figures include public production (roads, mail service, defense, the law, and so on), transfers (social security, unemployment benefits, and so forth), and servicing government debt. The overwhelming portion of that expenditure is financed by taxation.

One notable duty of government is to correct market failure. Stabilizing the macroeconomy (Chapter 4) is part of that duty. But communities can fail, too. Both markets and communities suffer from an inability to supply adequate levels of public goods; the rule of law, as opposed to the restraint of social norms, being a prominent example. Similarly, neither the market nor the community is able to restrict the production of public bads to the extent society would wish. Both institutions harbor externalities, be they beneficial or harmful. The role of the (ideal) state in each such case of institutional failure is clear enough.

Families can also fail. Although it may seem altogether too intrusive of the state to enter the family's domain, in Becky's world they do that regularly. And for good reason. Dysfunctional households in Desta's world are counseled by the community; but because there is often no community in their neighborhood, Becky's world no longer has that option. That's one reason why government social workers and counselors in Becky's world intervene on behalf of children against abusive adults and offer help to improve the behavior of destructive children.

Markets and communities are both inadequate for supplying merit goods. Some merit goods are private commodities (personal health), some are public goods (information about potential pandemics), while others lie somewhere in between, involving as they do externalities (information about the dangers of smoking). Communities and markets ought ideally to be supplemented by government measures when transactions involve merit goods. The government can do that by taxing households and firms and providing the merit goods either by producing them or by subsidizing their production in the private sector.

The Equality-Efficiency Trade-off

The allocations of goods and services realized in both markets and communities are shaped by the assets households have inherited from the past. It is a common complaint against markets that they harbor vast inequalities in wealth. In Becky's world that complaint has become urgent as the gap between the rich and the poor has increased greatly in recent decades. In the US, for example, the richest 10% of households in 1978 enjoyed 32% of GDP, whereas in 1998 the corresponding figure had risen to 41%. It is a complaint too in Becky's world that women suffer in the labor market relative to men. Earlier we noted that communities can also be rough on those who had the misfortune to inherit little and that they can be rough on women too. Visitors to communities may not notice those inequalities, but that's because in rural parts of Desta's world all people are very poor. Differences in wealth are reflected in the frequency and quality of their meals, the number of clothes they own, the quality of their bedding and kitchen utensils, and the durability of their homes (whether they are made of mud or brick). And women are often discreetly out of sight. None of those inequalities is quite as conspicuous as the ones visible in Becky's world today, but when households are desperately poor, small differences can be a matter

People displaced by Hurricane Katrina in 2005 seek temporary shelter in the New Orleans Superdome. Media coverage of Katrina's aftermath, including the displacement of the city's poorest residents, starkly revealed the extent of the American poverty gap.

of life and death. Which is why it is imprudent to wax lyrical about communities and rail against markets at the same time.

The distribution of goods and services is therefore a matter of government concern. However, if we revert to T. H. Marshall's three-way classification of well-being, it is an interesting fact that people today regard it axiomatic that everyone has an equal right to civil and political liberties, but don't make the same claim over the distribution of (inclusive) wealth. Why? It may be because generally speaking respecting the civil and political liberties of others doesn't cost anyone anything directly, whereas redistributing wealth costs those having to give up some of their wealth. The legal theorist Charles Fried has remarked that such aspects of civil rights as the right not to be interfered with in forbidden ways don't have natural limitations. ("If I am let alone, the commodity I obtain does not appear of its nature to be a scarce or limited one. How can we run out of people not harming each other, not lying to each other, leaving each other alone?") It is possible to honor civil rights, but it may not be possible to honor the right to health care: the economy may simply not have sufficient resources. The point is that, unlike wealth, democracy doesn't have to be created, it has only to be protected. The economist James Mirrlees was the first to show convincingly why in deliberating over distributions of wealth, we have to care about differences in individual talents to produce, worry about incentives and the concomitant notion of obligations (to honor agreements, not behave opportunistically, and so forth), consider people's needs, and take into account the related matter of deserts. An excessive government zeal to equalize wealth by means of taxes and subsidies could reduce household incentives to produce wealth to such an extent that everyone's interest is hurt. This is the classic equality-efficiency trade-off.

Market–Community Mediation

All societies rely on a mix of markets and communities. The mix shifts through changing circumstances, as people find ways to circumvent difficulties in realizing the benefits of cooperation. That communities help to make markets work should be a commonplace. No legal contract is air tight. There are incomplete specifications no matter how wily are the lawyers who have been called upon to draft them. A society that works well is a society that has a reached a tacit understanding of what are *reasonable expectations* about one another's dealings. Communities can play a big role in creating and sustaining reasonable expectations. They form the institution where households are able to deliberate matters and exchange information about the quality of market products and public services. Communities are also a place for political debate. They can discipline markets and government.

But they can also stifle the rise of markets. When ties are dense and intense, exit from communities is very costly. Someone wishing to "buy" his way out of his long-term relationships within his community and leave for the market place elsewhere wouldn't be able to do so if he faced risk that the community would seek retribution from those of his family he would be leaving behind. In an opposite vein, the growth of markets can destroy communities and make certain vulnerable groups worse off. If markets grow in nearby towns, those with lesser ties in villages (young men) are more likely to be able to take advantage of them and make a break with those customary obligations that are enshrined in prevailing social norms. Those with greater domestic attachments would notice this and reason that the expected benefits from complying with agreements are now lower (Chapter 2). Either way, social norms of reciprocity could be expected to weaken, making certain groups of people (women, the old, the very young) worse off. To put the matter in the language we have developed here, when people take their engagements away from communities to markets, the transfer gives rise to externalities. We don't read much about them in economic commentaries, because they are not run-of-the-mill externalities like industrial production degrading the local environment. But they are real externalities. One task of government is to identify them and find ways to soften the blow on those who get hurt by them.

In countries where the rule of law doesn't work well, where officials regard the public sphere to be their private domain, where markets are often absent, communities are what keep people alive. That's why many intellectuals today find them to be an attractive alternative to (impersonal) markets. But we need to bear in mind that communitarian obligations can check the growth of markets. Moreover, personal obligations inherited from the past can prevent public officials from acting dispassionately. What appears as corruption in Becky's world could be social obligation in Desta's world. Similarly, one man's civic association in Becky's world is another man's special interest group. These differences in perception are a source of cultural clashes that have led to societal tragedies. It isn't unusual in Desta's world for communities to pit themselves against one another, but rushing the streets with weapons haven't led to economic progress.

Democratic Voting Rules

In a well-ordered society civic education seeks to inculcate a sense of citizenship in people. When shopping, we don't need to know who needs what and why. Markets help to save enormously on information costs, permitting citizens not to worry about one another when going about their daily business in the market place (Chapter 4). But even ideal markets are effective only with regard to transactions in private goods. Citizens *should* worry about one another in the *public* sphere, which includes externalities, and the supply of public and merit goods such as the distribution of wealth and the rule of law. Civic awareness is to recognize and embrace the dichotomy between the private and public spheres of our lives.

On a day-to-day basis, the difference between the private and public spheres depends on the reach of government. The concern someone has toward the poor in a society where the state only maintains the rule of law and protects citizens from foreign aggression—the Minimal State—would be different from the concern she would have in a Welfare State, of the kind now prevalent in Western Europe. The reason is that in the Welfare State she faces additional taxation to finance redistribution; whereas, in the Minimal State, redistribution can only be achieved by means of voluntary transfers. She shouldn't have to worry about the poor in the Welfare State (it is the government's task to enforce redistributive measures). In contrast, she will be active on their behalf in the Minimal State. Since the choices she faces in the two societies differ greatly, she chooses differently.

In democratic societies, candidates standing for election represent public policies. So, in voting for a candidate one votes for a public policy, or more accurately, a set of probable policies. Since public policies influence the production and distribution of goods and services—we will call

A tank burns as Ethiopian rebels enter Addis Ababa in 1991, ending the regime of authoritarian ruler Mengistu Haile Mariam. Destructive forces such as war and revolution are powerful impediments to economic development.

them *outcomes* here—in voting for a candidate one votes for probable outcomes. Presumably, citizens differ in their interpretation of social well-being. If they do, they would rank candidates differently and therefore vote differently. But even if there was little disagreement among citizens over ethical values, their personal interests would typically differ, and it is most likely that they would differ in their beliefs about the way public policies influence outcomes. So citizens face the problem of combining their beliefs into an aggregate. Voting rules governing the selection of public officials aggregate citizens' ethical preferences. Formally, a *voting rule* is a method for choosing from a set of alternatives (for example, political candidates) on the basis of voters' *rankings* over those alternatives.

Why Voters Should Insist on Ranking All Candidates

Over the centuries people have devised many voting rules—majority rule, plurality rule, rank-order voting, unanimity rule, approval voting, instant run-off, and so on—and their advantages and drawbacks are not always apparent from casual inspection. Is there an ideal voting rule? We will study this question presently, but we should note at once that many national electoral systems are a far cry from being ideal because voters are required to record only their favorite candidate rather than rank them all. The problem with those systems is that they suppress information on how voters rank candidates who are *not* their favorite. If only two candidates compete, this limitation obviously makes no difference, but with three or more candidates, it can matter a great deal. To illustrate this (see Table 3 on page 194), imagine that there are three candidates—*A*, *B*, *C*—and that the electorate is divided into three groups.

Everyone in the first group, amounting to 30% of the electorate, ranks *A* over *B* and *B* over *C*, which we will write as (*A*, *B*, *C*). Among the second group, amounting to 36% of the electorate, the ranking is (*B*, *A*, *C*); among the remaining 34%, the ranking is (*C*, *A*, *B*). Consider an electoral system, such as the one governing French Presidential elections, where the voting rule dictates that if no candidate obtains an outright majority, the two candidates with the largest numbers of votes would face each other in a run-off. We will call the rule *plurality run-off*. In our example, *B* and *C*, with 36% and 34% of the top vote, respectively, would move forward into a run-off, where *B* would win easily because 66% of the electorate prefer him to *C*.

There is something obviously not right about that outcome. Candidate *A* commands an enormous majority: 64% of the electorate prefer *A* to *B*, and 66% prefer *A* to *C*. Surely, *A* should be elected. The underlying intuition here favors the *simple majority rule*, by which I mean a rule that requires voters to submit their rankings of all candidates and identifies the winner to be the one who beats each opponent in head-to-head competition based on these rankings.

Candidate ranking	% of voters choosing this ranking
(A,B,C)	30
(B,A,C)	36
(C,A,B)	34

Winning candidate under:

1. Plurality run-off: candidate B

2. Simple majority rule: candidate A

3. Rank-order rule: candiate A

Table 3. Comparison of voting rules

The problem with the kind of reasoning I have just deployed is that it is a prisoner of numerical examples. In some other situation, involving a larger number of candidates and a wider range of voters' rankings, perhaps some other voting rule would yield a more intuitively appealing winner than simple majority rule. In view of this, it would seem best to evaluate alternative voting rules in terms of fundamental ethical principles that any voting rule should satisfy. Kenneth Arrow originated this axiomatic approach to voting theory in a 1951 monograph that stands today as one of the great masterpieces in the humanities and social sciences. In what follows, I shall consider a set of ethical principles that, although they are not exactly the ones Arrow considered, are for our purposes here the same.

The Impossibility of an Ethically Ideal Voting Rule

What are those ethical principles? One would be the *consensus principle*, which states that if in everyone's judgment candidate *A* is better than candidate *B*, then *B* should not be elected. Another important principle holds that all voters should count equally, which can be translated as the "one-person one-vote," or equal-treatment principle. Economists call it the principle of *anonymity*, because it insists that who you are shouldn't determine your influence on the election.

A third principle has been named *neutrality*. It has two components. The first requires that the voting rule should not be biased in favor of any candidate (not even the incumbent!). The second requires that the choice made by the voting rule between candidates *A* and *B* shouldn't depend on voter's views about some third candidate *C*. The first component is clearly appealing in the present context, where the alternatives being voted on are candidates. (In other contexts, such as making an amendment to the US Constitution, the condition is violated because the status quo, the Constitution, is favored over all other alternatives.) To see the force of the second component, consider the *rank-order rule*. Under that rule, if, say, three candidates are competing, each voter assigns three points to his or her favorite, two to the next favorite, and one to the least favorite. The rule ranks candidates according to the total number of points each receives. It is easy to confirm that the rank-order rule satisfies the consensus principle and the principle of anonymity. But it runs into trouble with the neutrality principle. To see how, suppose that in the numerical example we have just studied, there are 100 voters. If the rank-order rule is applied to the election, candidate *A* would receive 230 points ($30 \times 3 + 36 \times 2 + 34 \times 2$); *B* would receive 202 points ($30 \times 2 + 36 \times 3 + 34 \times 1$); and *C* would receive 168 points ($30 \times 1 + 36 \times 1 + 34 \times 3$). It follows that under the rank-order rule the candidates would be ranked as, *A* over *B* and *B* over *C*. But suppose the 36 voters who had earlier ranked the candidates (*B*, *A*, *C*) had a second thought and ranked them instead as (B, C, A). Candidate A would now receive 194 points $(30 \times 3 + 36 \times 1 + 34 \times 2)$; B would continue to receive 202 points $(30 \times 2 + 36 \times 3 + 34 \times 1)$; and C would receive 204 points $(30 \times 1 + 36 \times 2 + 34 \times 3)$. The candidates would now be ranked as, C over B and B over A. Notice however that the 36 voters changed their mind only over the relative merits of candidates A and C: candidate B remained their favorite. Despite that, the rank-order rule altered the relative placements of B and C. This shows that the rule can't be guaranteed to satisfy the second component of the neutrality principle.

In contrast, the simple majority rule satisfies the consensus principle, anonymity, and neutrality no matter what are the voters' rankings over candidates. Unfortunately, the rule falls foul of a fourth principle: *transitivity*. Transitivity requires that if a voting rule ranks candidate A over B and B over C, then A should be ranked over C. To confirm that simple majority rule is not always transitive, consider the situation we have just discussed, namely, where 30% of the electorate rank the candidates A, B, and C as (A, B, C), 36% as (B, C, A), and 34% as (C, A, B). The simple majority rule ranks A over B because 64% of the voters rank A over B and it ranks B over C because 66% rank B over C. Transitivity says that the rule should be required to rank A over C. But 70% of the voters rank C over A, which implies that the simple majority rule is obliged to rank C over A. We have a contradiction here, a possibility that was identified in the late eighteenth century by the Marquis de Condorcet. The example is now known in economics literature as the Condorcet paradox.

Is this pure theory or is transitivity violated by the simple majority rule in real life? Political scientists have explored this question by studying decisions reached in US Congress. To see how they have gone about their investigation, let us return to the previous example, but now rename the alternatives as bills proposed in US Congress. Say *A* is the bill being proposed in Congress and *B* and *C* are amendments to the bill. Suppose that instead of members of Congress being asked to rank the three alternatives, the rule is to vote first on *A* and *B*, and then vote on the winner of that contest and *C*. Under the simple majority rule, *A* would win in the first contest (64% of the voters favor *A* over *B*); in the second round, *C* would beat *A* (70% favor *C* over *A*). Consequently *C* would be chosen. Now suppose instead that members of Congress are asked first to vote on *A* and *C* and then vote on the winner of that contest and *B*. Under the simple majority rule, *C* would win the first contest (70% favor *C* over *A*), but in the second round *B* would beat *C* (66% of the voters favor *B* over *C*, remember). The outcome depends on the order in which pairs of alternatives are presented to voters: the agenda matters. It is easy to check that the agenda would not matter in those situations where the voting rule satisfies transitivity. Political scientists studying outcomes of votes in US Congress have discovered that the agenda does seem to matter on occasion. When it does, it is a sign that transitivity is violated by the voting rule.

The simple majority rule and the rank-order rule are but two voting rules. The question arises whether there is *some* voting rule that can be relied upon to satisfy the consensus principle, anonymity, neutrality, and transitivity no matter what the voters' rankings over candidates happen to be. Arrow's "impossibility theorem" says that if the number of alternatives exceeds two, the answer is "no." The theorem holds that if the alternatives number three or more, *all* voting rules must sometimes violate at least one of the four ethical principles. (If the alternatives

This view of the US Capitol shows the building's west façade. While ideal voting systems, governments, and markets are impossible to achieve, civic awareness and responsibility *are* possible and essential to humanitarian achievements in today's world.

are two, Arrow's theorem doesn't apply. For example, the simple majority rule satisfies all four ethical criteria no matter what the voters' preferences happen to be. Transitivity doesn't apply because the criterion has force only when there are three or more alternatives.)

The result is both deep and depressing. There is no way out of the dilemma but to drop one of the principles. Of the four, the neutrality principle has come up for the greatest scrutiny among economists. The principle insists that the *only* information a voting rule should be allowed to use is each voter's ranking of candidates. However, no one has provided evidence of what additional information could be made permissible at a polling station without jeopardizing the electoral process. Making comparisons of voters' ethical "feelings"? It would no doubt violate the neutrality principle and provide a way out of Arrow's paradox, but who is to make the comparisons and why should anyone trust the person making them? It seems to me, we simply have to live with Arrow's theorem and do the best we can. Let us then say that a voting rule *works well* for a class of rankings of candidates if it satisfies the four ethical axioms when all voters' rankings belong to that class. It can be shown that whenever a voting rule works well, so does the simple majority rule. Furthermore, the simple majority rule works well in some cases in which other voting rules do not. Condorcet's paradox notwithstanding, the simple majority rule would appear to be the most robust of all voting rules. So, one compromise that suggests itself is to adopt the simple majority rule; with the proviso that, if no candidate in an election obtains a simple majority against all opponents, then among those who defeat the most opponents in head-to-head comparisons, the winner is the one with the highest rank-order score.

Just as circles can't be squared, ideal voting rules don't exist, ideal markets are a pleasant myth, and ideal governments can't be conjured up because governments are run by people. If all this feels overly depressing, let us acknowledge that the human losses we see round us aren't due to any of these analytical difficulties. Stunted and wasted lives aren't caused by the "impossibility theorems" I have reported in this monograph. They happen because people have yet to learn how to live with one another.

EPILOGUE

●

I HAVE USED BECKY'S AND DESTA'S experiences to show you how it can be that the lives of essentially very similar persons can become so different and remain so different. Desta's life is one of poverty. In her world people don't enjoy food security, don't own many assets, are stunted and wasted, don't live long, can't read or write, aren't empowered, can't insure themselves well against crop failure or household calamity, don't have control over their own lives, and live in unhealthy surroundings. Each deprivation reinforces the others, so that the productivity of labor effort, ideas, manufactured capital, and of land and natural resources are all very low and remain low. Desta's life is filled with *problems* each day.

An example of Becky's world helping Desta's by supporting local enterprises is the aid agency Relief International's micro-loan program for women affected by Iran's 2003 earthquake. A local woman, shown baking bread, has received a loan to buy cows, and she provides for her family with the milk she sells.

Becky suffers from no such deprivation. She faces what her society calls *challenges*. In her world, the productivity of labor effort, ideas, manufactured capital, and of land and natural resources are all very high and continually increasing. Success in meeting each challenge reinforces the prospects of success in meeting further challenges.

We have seen, however, that despite the enormous differences between Becky's and Desta's lives, there is a unified way to view them, and that economics is an essential language for analyzing them. It is no doubt tempting to pronounce that life's essentials can't be reduced to mere economics, but I hope I have convinced you that economic reasoning is essential if we are to make sense of the bewildering variety of ways people everywhere try to make something of their lives. That some succeed while others fail is to be expected. What economics shows us is that neither personal failure nor personal success is entirely a matter of personal effort and luck. Success and failure lie at the intersection of the personal and the social. Of course, to say that is easy enough, but to uncover the pathways by which the personal and the social interact is immensely hard. I have tried to show you that it can nevertheless be done, and that without an understanding of those pathways, debates over national and international policies are unfruitful.

I am resisting the temptation to produce a list of the material things Desta needs, partly because they are all too obvious, but partly also because they serve only to satisfy proximate needs. That Becky's world shouldn't create roadblocks in Desta's (through trade restrictions, domestic agricultural subsidies, and so on) is also obvious and proximate. What is neither obvious nor proximate—the elusive bird we would all wish to catch for Desta—is for communities in her world to discover how to shape new avenues to do business with one another so as to increase their inclusive wealths.

In a moving discourse on the character of poverty at the 2001 Plenary Meeting of the Pontifical Academy of Social Sciences, Vatican, Justice Nicholas McNally of Zimbabwe urged us all to see poverty as a sense of fatalism to ever-increasing economic hardships in a changing, and elsewhere an often progressive, world. At that same meeting, the political scientist Wilfrido Villacorta suggested that the term "poor" when applied to countries is perhaps no longer useful; that countries ought perhaps now to be classified in accordance with some such term as "progressive," so that we may ask if they have the institutions, policies, and civic attitudes in place to enable people to improve their lot. Perhaps the best Becky's world can do for Desta's is to offer financial and technical assistance so as to promote and support local enterprises—including those involving education and primary health care—that people there are all too keen to create even as they see from a distance how people elsewhere have been able to improve their conditions of living. And perhaps the best Desta's world can do for Becky's is to alert it to the enormous stresses economic growth there has put on Nature. There is, alas, no magic potion for bringing about economic progress in either world.

FURTHER READING

•

Political Economy, by Edmund Phelps (Norton, 1985) and *Economics*, by Joseph Stiglitz and Carl Walsh (Norton, 2006) are fine introductory textbooks.

CHAPTER ONE

On economic growth, see *The Mystery of Economic Growth*, by Elhanan Helpman (Belknap, 2004).

CHAPTER TWO

On trust, see *Trust: Making and Breaking Cooperative Relations*, edited by Diego Gambetta (Blackwell, 1988) and *Social Capital: A Multifaceted Perspective*, edited by Partha Dasgupta and Ismail Serageldin (World Bank, 2000). Good introductions to the theory of games are *Fun and Games*, by Ken Binmore (Heath, 1992) and *Games, Strategies, and Managers*, by John McMillan (Oxford University Press, 1993).

CHAPTER THREE

An Inquiry into Well-Being and Destitution, by Partha Dasgupta (Clarendon, 1993) offers a more detailed account of communities.

CHAPTER FOUR

On markets, see *Microeconomic Theory and Applications*, by Edgar Browning and Mark Zupan (Addison Wesley, 1998). On the macroeconomic consequences of market failure, see *Macroeconomics*, by N. Gregory Mankiw (Worth, 2000).

CHAPTER FIVE
On the economics of knowledge, see the essays in *The Economics of Science and Innovation*, edited by Paula Stephan and David Audretsch (Edward Elgar, 2000).

CHAPTER SIX
On households, see *A Treatise on the Family*, by Gary Becker (Chicago University Press, 1981).

CHAPTER SEVEN
On the economics of natural capital, see *Human Well-Being and the Natural Environment*, by Partha Dasgupta (Oxford University Press, 2001).

CHAPTER EIGHT
On the role of the state, see *Economics of the Public Sector*, by Joseph Stiglitz (Norton, 2000). The classic on collective choice is *Social Choice and Individual Values*, by Kenneth Arrow (Wiley, 1951; 2nd edn, 1963). *Collective Choice and Social Welfare*, by Amartya Sen (North Holland, 1979) contains a wide-ranging discussion of collective choice and its place in social life. The exposition in Chapter 8 has been taken from "The Fairest Vote of All," by Partha Dasgupta and Eric Maskin, *Scientific American* (March 2004).

I have not included any account of the history of my discipline because I am inexpert on the subject. Readers wishing to learn the history of economic thought should study *Epochs of Economic Theory*, by Amiya Dasgupta (Blackwell, 1985).

INDEX

•

Page numbers in *italics* include illustrations and photographs/captions.

adverse selection, 88, 99, 107
Africa, sub-Saharan, *57*
   economic development in, 168,
     170, 171, 173
   environment/ecology affecting, 163
   gender inequality in, 128
   incomes in, 3–5, 20, 21
   rearing children in, 129–30, *131*
   standard of living in, 2–5, *4*
   TFR in, 27
agreements, 40–45, 47, 49–59, 99
agriculture, *24*
   Fertile Crescent and, *16*–17
   gender inequality and, 128
   piece rates in, 116
   risks in, 132, 133
   subsistence, 5, 27, 50, 68, *89*
Amnesty International, 85
Argentina, 21
Aristotle, 114
Arrow, Kenneth, 64, *65*, 117, 194, 198
Aumann, Robert, 52
Australia, 22

Bangladesh, 168, *170*
bankruptcy, 142, 143
banks, 2, 3, 85, *136*
bargaining, 40, 184

barter, 68–69
Bauer, Peter, 175
Bear Stearns, *62*
Becker, Gary, 25
bifurcations, 56
biomass-based economies, 22
Boserup, Esther, 128
Brazil, 21, 50
Brundtland Commission Report, 159

capital
   assets, 59, 160, 163–66
   human, 25, 26, 29, 100, 160, 166,
     167
   manufactured, 23, 29, 30, 160,
     166, 167
   natural, 150–51, 160, 166, 167,
     172, 173
   opportunity cost of, 155
   working, 46, 53, 82
Central America, 21
Chen, Lincoln, 127
China, *ii*–iv, *87*, 128, *163*, 168, *170*,
   172
civil liberties, 176, 177, 179, 180, 188
Coalbrookdale by Night (Loutherbourg),
   11
commodities. *see* goods and services

common property resources (CPRs)
    affecting fertility, 130
    governments affecting, 56
    large households affecting, 141–42
    property rights and, 60–63, *61*
    trust affecting, *38*–39
communities, *80*–89
    goods and, 66–67, 186
    markets and, 59–60, 189–90
    network of, 85–89
    non-cooperation affecting, 56
    rebuilding, 57–*58*
    social norms affecting, 177
    tied engagements in, 82–85
    weak/strong ties, 86–*89*
competition, 79, 98, 101, 102, 104
Condorcet, Marquis de, 196, 199
consumption, 139–40, 155–58
cooperation, 51–62, 81
corruption, 34–*37*, *35*, 48, 56, *62*
cost of living, 1–5, 19
credit, 2, 48, 49
critical mass, 78
culture, 4, 44, 75–79

Daily, Gretchen, 150
David, Paul A., 118
Diamond, Jared, 17–18, 33
discount rates, 52, 155–57
double-coincidence of wants, 69

ecology. *see* environment/ecology
econometrics, 12, 13
economic development
    democracy and, 177–79
    environment and, *146*–48, 151–*59*
    GDP/productive base and, 159–63,
      166, 169, 171–73
    HDI and, 171

    natural capital and, 150–51
    population growth affecting, 169
    sustainable, 163–73, *170*
    total factor productivity affecting,
      169
    war/revolution affecting, *192*
economies of scale, 104–6, 142
education, 2, 3, 23, 26, 67
efficiency, *30*, 102, 103, 144, 186, 189
Ehrlich, Paul, 150
enforcement, 46–59, *47*
English Statute of Monopolies, 120
environment/ecology, *32*, 150–51,
    161–*63*
    affecting rural poor, 22, 56, *57*
    biomassed-based economies
      affecting, 22
    carbon emissions affecting, 8, 62,
      67, 148, 154–55, 157, 167
    climate change and, 153–59
    deforestation and, *57*, 152, *153*, 161
    natural capital and, 150–51
    population growth affecting, 26
    strip mining and, *149*
    urban sprawl affecting, *146*–47
equilibrium
    competitive, 95–96, 101, 102
    cooperation and, 57
    market, 93, 101
    Nash, 41–42, 51, 55
    supply and demand affecting, 95,
      96, 99
    TFRs and, 76
    trust and, 59
Ethiopia, 2, 20, *37*, *89*
Eurasia, 17–18, 118
externalities, 66–68, 161–62

fertility, *24*, 26–27, 128–30

firms, 88, 92–98, 105–6, 142–45, *143*
Fisher, Irving, 139
Fogel, Robert, 33
Ford Motor Company, *30*
forecasts/predictions, 6, 10, *14*, 110, 157, 167
France, 109
free-riding problem, 67–68, 103–4, 130
free trade, 151–53
Fried, Charles, 188
Fudenberg, Drew, 52

game theory, 40, *41*, 53
gender inequality, 3, 23, 27, *28*, 61, 127–29, 186–87
Germany, *70*, 109, 119
goods and services
    classifications of, 63–65
    determinants and, 180–81
    distribution of, 102, 103, 188
    durable, 113
    egalitarian, 103
    excludable, 120
    markets for, 92
    merit, 181–84, *182–83*, 186
    money as, 68–71
    ownership of, 60–63
    prices of, 92, 99, 107, 110
    private, 66–68, 92, 120
    public, 66–68, 103, *112*–13, 185
    supply and demand affecting, 93–95, *94*, 109–10
    well-being and, 180
Goody, Jack, 118
government(s). *see also* institutions
    authoritarianism and, 177, 178, 184, *192*
    backing money, 69, *70*
    corruption in, *24*, 34–*37*, *35*, 56

    democratic, 176–79, 181
    enforcing agreements and, *47*, 48–49
    equalizing wealth, 188–89
    freedom and, 176–79
    free press affecting, 48–49
    functions of, 175–76, 185–91
    liberties and, 176, 177, 179, 180, 188
    markets and, 103, 186
    Minimal States of, 191
    voting rules in, 191–99, *194*
    Welfare States of, 191
grim strategy, 53, 54, 55, 82–84
gross domestic product (GDP)
    economic development and, 159–63
    enforcing agreements and, *47*
    environment/ecology and, 161–63
    HDI and, 161, 162
    measuring, 18–22
    population affecting, 30
    sustainable development, 147
    TFR affecting, 31
    trust and, 59

Harsanyi, John, 41
Hayek, Friedrich von, 98
health care, 25, 67, 126, 127, 128
Hirschman, Albert, 86
Holdren, John, 150
household(s), *x–1*
    borrowing/saving/investing, 134–42, *140*
    definition of, 126
    extended families in, *124*–25, 126, *131*
    failure of, 185–86
    food distribution in, 126, 127
    gender inequality in, 127–29

insurance and, 130–34
nuclear family in, *124*–25
property rights/fertility and, 129–30
wealth of, 1–5, *2*, 96, 97, 100
human capital
adverse affecting economic growth, 29
commodities as, 100
definition of, 25
reducing cost of, 26
Human Development Index (HDI), 22, *24*, 161, 162, 171

inclusive investment, 166–71
income, 19, 20, 21, 59, 68, 79
India, 21–22, 61, *80*–81, 127–28, 168, *170*
Industrial Revolution, *11*
institutions, 34–*37*, *35*, 46–59, *47*, 61, 74, 113–23. *see also* government(s)
insurance
adverse selection in, 88
government and, 133, *134*
moral hazard in, 88
risk, 130–31
in sub-Saharan Africa, 3, 35, 39, 49, 59, 81, 135
Intergovernmental Panel on Climate Change (IPCC), 153
International Monetary Fund, *168*
inventions/discoveries, *112*–13, 115, 116, *119*, 120
Iran, *174*–75
Italy, 84, 118

Japan, 21, 109

Kalecki, Michal, 111
Keynes, John Maynard, *9*, 111

Landes, David, 33
Lange, Oscar, 98
laws/norms, 45–46
anti-trust, 104, *105*
external enforcement of, 46–49
mutual enforcement of, 49–59
Leibnitz, Gottfried Wilhelm von, 118
Lerner, Abba, 98
Limited Liability Act, 145
Lindahl, Erik, 63–64, 65
Lipset, Seymour Martin, 177
literacy, 22, 23, *24*, 67
long-term relationships, 51–59, 74, 86, 88
Loutherbourg, Philip Jakob, *11*
Lubchenco, Jane, 150

macroeconomics, *14*, 18–22, 33–37, 58, 107
Maddison, Angus, 19–20
Mariam, Mengistu Haile, *192*
market(s), *90*–91, *106*
communities and, 59–60, 189–90
competition in, 101, 102, 104
efficiency of, 97, 102
equilibrium, 101
failure, 91, 103–11
fluctuations, 107–11
government and, 103, 185
Great Depression and, *108*
ideal, 91–102
infrastructure and, 106–7
interdependent, 99–102
missing, 69, 71, 100, 161
monopoly, 104–7, *105*
Pareto-efficient, 102, 103
prices, 19, 93, 96, 161–62
supply and demand affecting, 93–95, *94*, 99

Marshall, Alfred, 95, 99
Marshall, T. H., 176, 179, 180, 188
Maskin, Eric, 52
Matson, Pamela, 150
McNally, Justice Nicholas, 203
Meade, James, 111
Medawar, Peter, 117
Mirrlees, James, 188
models, economic, 10, 11–*14*, 41, 69, 72
money, 68–71, *70*
monopolies, 104–7, *105*, 120
Mooney, Harold, 150
moral hazard, 88, 99, 107, 115, 116, 144
Musgrave, Richard, 181

Nash, John Forbes, *41*
national defense, 66, 67
Newton, Isaac, 118
New York Stock Exchange, *143*, 144
North, Douglass, 33

Ohlin, Bertil, 111
On the Nature of Metals, *119*

Pakistan, *47*, 168–*72*, *170*
Pareto, Vilfredo, 102
partnerships, 39, 53, 82–83
patent system, *112*–13, *119*, 120
Pigou, A. C., 68
Plenary Meeting of the Pontifical Academy of Social Sciences, 203
population, *7*, *24*, 26, 30, 148, 169, 172
poverty, 201–3
    affecting HDI, 22
    gap, *x*–5, 29, 186, *187*
    history of, 19–20

literacy and, 23
traps, 29
World Bank reducing, *21*
prices, 8, 19, 93, 99, 161–62, 165–67, 184
property rights, 60–63, 129–30
Protestant Ethic and the Spirit of Capitalism (Weber), *72*
punishment, 48–50, 53–55, 84

Ramsey, Frank, 139
Raven, Peter, 150
reciprocity, 39, 44, 49, 131
Relief International, *200*–201
Royal Society of London, 118
Rubinstein, Ariel, 52
rules/regulations
    of behavior, 51, 52
    corruption affecting, 36
    environment/ecology, 35
    grim strategy of, 53, 54, 55
    of law, 45, 177, 178
    of priority, 116–17, 118

Samuelson, Paul, 66, 69, 111, 115
Schelling, Thomas, 41
Schultz, Theodore, 25
science/technology, *25*, 26, 113–23, *119*
Selten, Reinhard, 41
Shapley, Lloyd, 52
Singapore, 178
slavery, *32*
Smith, Adam, 71
social
    capital, 37
    choice theory, *65*
    contracts, 40, 47, 49–50
    cost-benefit analysis, 185

disposition, 44–45
-economic liberties and, 176
influential behavior, 75–79
norms, 45, 50, 51, 54, 177
well-being, 164, 165, 179–85
Solow, Robert, *14*, 29
South East Asia, 21
standard of living, 2–5, *4*, 12–13,
    22–26, 108, 148
statistics, 11–12, 13, 43
Stiglitz, Joseph, 110
supply and demand, 93–96, *94*, 99,
    109–10

taxes, 2, 68
Tobin, James, 111
Tokyo Stock Exchange, *90*–91
total factor productivity, *30*, 31, 37,
    59, 169
total fertility rate (TFR), 26–27, 75, *76*
transactions
    anonymous, 70
    CPRs and, 61
    money for, 68, 70
    personal/impersonal, 85
    rules governing, 48
    verifiable, 51, 93, 107
trust, mutual
    communities/markets and, 59–60
    culture and, 71–79
    goods/services and, 63–71, *64*
    laws/norms and, 45–59, *47*
    money and, 68–71
    mutual affection and, 43–44
    property rights and, 60–63, *61*
    social disposition and, 44–45,
        75–79

United Kingdom, 31, 109, 168, *170*, 173
United Nations Development
    Programme (UNDP), 22
United States
    average income in, 20
    Capitol Building, *198*
    economic development in, 168, *170*
    Federal Reserve, *136*
    inclusive investment in, 173
    Patent Office, *112*–13
    unemployment rate in, 109

Venezuela, 21
Vietnam, *58*
Villacorta, Wilfrido, 203
virtuous/vicious cycles, 29
Visaria, Pravin, 127
voting rules, 191–99, *194*

water, 3, 24, *38*–39, 63–*64*
Watkins, Susan Cotts, 78
wealth, 19, 96–97, 100, 166, 184,
    188–89
Weber, Max, *72*
well-being, 164, 165, 179–85, *182–83*
White, Harry Dexter, *9*
Wicksell, Knut, 66, 115
work force
    contracts, 115
    division of labor in, 1–3, *4*, 71, 126
    Great Depression and, *108*
    performance bonuses in, 116
    unemployment and, 110
    women in, 1, 27, 186
World Bank, 19, *21*, *24*, 167, *168*,
    169, 172
World Values Survey, 72–73, 74

PICTURE CREDITS

•

SHUTTERSTOCK: x: © Shutterstock/Pichugin Dmitry (top); © Shutterstock/Sir Armstrong (bottom); 37: © Shutterstock/ akva; 38: © Shutterstock/Kang Khoon Seang; 57: © Shutterstock/ Mike VON BERGEN; 62: © Shutterstock/Derrick Salters; 106: © Shutterstock/Klaus Sailer; 136: © Shutterstock/Jonathan Larsen; 146: © Shutterstock/iofoto; 149: © Shutterstock/Erik Patton; 153: © Shutterstock/Dr. Morley Read

COURTESY WIKIMEDIA COMMONS: 11: Philipp Jakob Loutherbourg d. J. 003/Philipp Jakob Loutherbourg d. J./London Science Museum; 21: The World Bank Group building/Author: AgnosticPreachersKid; 58: Burning Viet Cong base camp/US Archiv ARCWEB; 64: Libyen-oasel/Author: Sfivat; 70: 500000 Mark Altenburg 1923 front/Altenburg; 72: Die protestantische Ethik und der 'Geist' des Kapitalismus original cover/http://etext.lib.virginia.edu/etcbin/ toccer-reldem?id=WebProt.xml&images=images/modeng&data=/ texts/german&tag=public&part=front; 119: De re metallica p 391/ Author: Georgius Agricola; 134: Katrina-14512/FEMA; 144: NYSE127/Author: Ryan Lawler; 172: Ogdclofficeislamabad/Author: Azamishaque; 198: Capitol Building Full View/Author: noclip

BRIEF INSIGHTS

•

A series of concise, engrossing, and enlightening books that explore every subject under the sun with unique insight.

Available now or coming soon:

THE AMERICAN PRESIDENCY

ARCHITECTURE

ATHEISM

THE BIBLE

BUDDHISM

CHRISTIANITY

CLASSICAL MYTHOLOGY

CLASSICS

CONSCIOUSNESS

THE CRUSADES

ECONOMICS

EXISTENTIALISM

GALILEO

GANDHI

GLOBALIZATION

HISTORY

INTERNATIONAL RELATIONS

JUDAISM

KAFKA

LITERARY THEORY

LOGIC

MACHIAVELLI

MARX

MATHEMATICS

MODERN CHINA

MUSIC

NELSON MANDELA

PAUL

PHILOSOPHY

PLATO

POSTMODERNISM

RENAISSANCE ART

RUSSIAN LITERATURE

SEXUALITY

SHAKESPEARE

SOCIAL AND CULTURAL ANTHROPOLOGY

SOCIALISM

STATISTICS

THE TUDORS

THE VOID